How To Live As One   by Frances Micklem

Contents

Introduction

This book takes the reader from an old to a new paradigm way of thinking. The old has long been characterized by the perspective that we are individuals and the new is grounded on the understanding that we are all one.

In order to learn to think in a different way, I will first provide a guide to identifying and clearing the deep sense of inevitability that stands in the way. I will then show how the geometry and general observance of nature supports this journey. This may be because nature is calling out for a rise in consciousness, by bringing us rapidly into crises, both personal and global.

A perspective that acknowledges that life is connected, brings with it a responsibility to recognize your own part. Therefore I have outlined ways to practice being honest and present with yourself, for others and your environment. As much of the world and many of the people in it will still be reflecting back the chaos created to date, I have included a section on shortcuts to oneness. These can help when you are triggered back to divisive ideas.

The training is to simultaneously expand your awareness and compassion. In this sense it is a healing journey, which comes with a guarantee: A person, who comes to know that they are a part of everything, has infinite power to draw on. He or she will need this power plus considerable mental discipline, to break free from the habitual identification with their separateness. If you make it, you can do anything. The final section is, therefore, devoted to developing your vision, directing your creative energy and achieving clarity of intention. The dialectic will then be complete.

Chapter One

Growth and freedom

Are you willing to look at your life and take responsibility for what you have created? In the past, we couldn't look. Each person found a focus to fuel their avoidance. Some argued they had not got time or had unsupportive friends and family. Some said they were not well enough and wanted to improve their physical health first. People have now come to accept that, in fact, everything happens first in our non physical energy fields. Situations and problems in our health and finances have been building up in our emotional and mental fields long before they manifest in the physical. Spiritual bankruptcy always precedes actual dereliction. So it is at the deepest level, after all, that we must start. You must be willing to go there to come back truly in one piece.

This unconscious, shadowy side which is so instrumental in our experience is not all bad. Yes, it holds the pain and fear that makes us not want to investigate. It holds our extensive predispositions to illness. However, it also holds all our creativity, unconditional love, potential and innate knowledge. We are energetic beings fired by spirit and thought, feeling and everything around us. I urge you to start considering your energetic existence as it has many plusses. We each have a full spectrum of energetic frequencies to tap into. From bliss to despair, from compassion to rage, from genius to ignorance. From birth, we wrongly start to identify with a limited few of these and decide that is who we are. The good news is that, underlying all the polarities of zeniths and nadirs, there is still this one warm sea. You might call it oneness or an underlying stillness or all that there is. You will see how to return everything to this peaceful fabric of energy. Instead of stress manifesting as illness or chaos, you heal it. The power of intention is enough.

To be sure you have cleared part of the energy spectrum, the divining method is second to none. In the past, a pendulum was used to identify. It was reliable at getting a yes or no answer to previously unknowable topics such as 'Will she have a colt or filly foal?' and 'How deep should we drill, to meet a clear water spring?' In this healing context, however, the swinging of the pendulum offers both identification of a problem area and shows the dissipation of the turbulence. When you start, you can safely assume that healing would be valuable in every area, so do not get stuck looking for subtle movements and clear answers. Simply start swinging the pendulum and when it naturally slows, trust that that is one aspect cleared. Bear in mind that the biggest risk in life is that you remain an unconscious, self fulfilling prophecy. This means you do not serve yourself well by just exploring your current reality. The way you formulate your questions changes from 'Will I get the job?' to 'Can I clear any obstacles to me getting the job?' or even 'Will this disease kill me?' to 'Can I clear the source of this illness and heal?' You are moving yourself into alignment with a better outcome, rather than just identifying what is probable, from your current perspective. The process you will go through, as you read this book, is to clear yourself and put in place constructive ways of thinking that will manifest continual positive results.

You will start by noticing the arbitrary parameters you have been working within. These may be ideas or beliefs that keep you small or archetypes that sabotage your conscious efforts. You will also become aware of how your environment, both in the land and the buildings you frequent, is impacting on your health. As you bring each turbulence you meet back into the underlying stillness, your health will improve. Instead of bracing yourself for the next thing you will have to deal with, you will come to relish the new capacity to heal situations and not fear them. You will start to literally resonate at a new frequency, with less and less resistance and conflict. As you detox energetically, the infinite organizing power of nature will help rearrange external reality to reflect your new equilibrium. The ripple effect of conscious thoughts and actions has great applications for global matters like world peace and the environment. Conscious thoughts and actions are characterized by feelings of joy, enthusiasm and acceptance, acceptance being the last resort if you are really challenged. All other energies take the good out of your reality, guilt being the lowest energy of all.

Chapter Two

Inevitability - Predispositions to illness

It is crucial to clear your sense of inevitability first. Inevitably takes shape in all sorts of beliefs in your mind that result in an engrained, victim dynamic throughout your life experience. This is because, with inevitably, you presuppose that you are powerless to change your self or outer landscape. You also reaffirm to yourself, repeatedly, that life is just happening to you, your participation is not making a significant difference. You also externalize all responsibility for your health and actions. You assume that your beliefs are true, evidenced facts about reality. This assumption makes it impossible to address them, or any issues, successfully because you have given them too much credibility and solidity and cannot let them go.

The clearing process starts with noticing what you believe already. Getting even one moment's objectivity - for example, 'oh look, I totally believe that my health is going to deteriorate each year until I become totally decrepit in old age' - allows you to use discernment - 'I do not want to make that a self fulfilling prophecy!' and also expand your horizons, using positively framed questions - 'what if...I grow old gracefully, enjoying the active and quiet phases of my life'. 'What if...I am still surfing, traveling the world and surrounded by people who love me, in my twilight years'. These things are possible, all these things can happen. Currently you believe what you have always believed, maybe what you were told or maybe ideas that you were born with or think you worked out for yourself.

Predispositions to illness are one such inevitability that it is important to deal with. The way to deal with them is to bring the light of awareness to them. See them for what they really are. We think of predispositions to illness as knowledge of our family and genetic make up. Medical records confirm things like, 'there is diabetes in the family' or 'a history of heart problems'. The reason we perpetuate problems generation after generation is not that these problems are infectious or genetically guaranteed. It is because we include ourselves in the problem. We identify with it. Think of statements you make like 'we all have bad knees'... or 'bad backs'... or 'a weak bladder'. Or, my father had it and one or two of my grand parents had it, so I'll probably have it'. You are assuming its yours, unconsciously or consciously fearing its arrival and, unfortunately, thus giving it sufficient energy to take physical shape in your own system. You also give a potential illness power by describing it as genetic or inherited.

I encourage you to remind yourself of this: We change what we consciously observe. This goes for cellular, genetic and family habits as well as anything else. So notice the tendencies - that is all they are - and set the intention to dissipate the disturbance back into oneness - be it a pain, a conflict, or a memory. Then pluck out of the universal stream of energy something like

6

'genetic structural integrity' or set your cellular receptor sites to only recognize health, or pay attention to the healthy choices you have made, rather than take on a family past riddled with mishap, illness or tragedy that was not really yours anyway. Predispositions to illness are a good place to start in your journey to self awareness generally as you can readily hear yourself go on about them. It is actually entertaining, too, to diffuse and stop this destructive running commentary we have tormented ourselves with for years.

There is always an underlying event that brought an affliction into the first family member, maybe generations ago. Say to yourself, 'whatever that was, usually an unacknowledged grief, I acknowledge it now with compassion and wish to release its vibrational hold'. If you don't, the root of the illness remains stored and is building up momentum to manifest in your life or in the next most susceptible member of your clan. Sometimes the symbolic source of illness and predispositions to illness are broader; started in a whole generation who endured war for example or starvation. Time spent in the conscious acknowledgement and release of those dark times, sends a ripple of healing to the whole world. Do not feel you have to hold difficult memories in your heart out of respect, either. We are clearing only the emotional charge around them, taking away the attachment, the drama and the perpetuation of trauma. You are allowing disturbed spiritual traces to pass on, so those you grieve for are in fact benefiting rather than being forgotten.

Inevitability - Soul Loss

Most of the people you meet have come through many life experiences and their souls are damaged. Often lost altogether. In the past, soul loss was considered the primary cause of death, above any illness or accident. Nowadays, it is only alluded to by the term 'losing the will to live'. So this is not occasional or only happening to people who get mixed up working with spiritual forces. It is commonplace and I would guarantee that if you ask about your own, you will find some part missing, awol, stolen, lost, exchanged or splintered. I recommend retrieving it at your earliest convenience. DIY (Do it yourself) is the only way. You will need to prepare yourself to trek off, to negotiate. Many people think they cannot or are fearful. You have to get empowered, right away. The order of events for DIY soul retrieval is first to imagine yourself surrounded by comrades, for the transition between worlds that you will have to make.

Dowse to see how many parts the soul is in. Then to find where they are. It may be the underworld, where there is a lot of darkness and they tend to covet the light. Here one has to be firm. It may be in purgatory where there are countless lost souls, which you will probably see as shadows. The work to do here is to clear all you meet. Then they will bring you what you are there to collect. Then there is Olympia, the seat of the Gods. The likelihood is that you will have negotiated your soul in a previous existence to save someone you loved or save your own skin. Happily, at the moment, these divinities have stopped competing with each other and have expressly said that we need as much light on earth at the moment as possible. It means they will give you your soul back, literally on request. Parts can also be left with or stolen by individuals. You do not need to find out who or when. Just visualize the meeting and asking for your soul to be returned. Clear for everyone you meet to go to the light or be at peace. Clear all attachments to you and vice versa.

This process has an epic ripple effect as you are clearing so many spirits and old contracts at once. When you have retrieved all the pieces, clear any resistance to accepting them back in to your body. I heard that it is very painful because of having been without it so long, but we have the tools to clear our resistance and accept whatever it brings. No doubt you will have interesting dreams and some deep changes. Just go with it and remember that now at last you have the chance to live fully. The habit of giving your energy away will be harder to change. Therefore, when you feel yourself very low, check in that you have not parted with your soul again. Keep bringing it back until it feels at home, appreciated and commits to staying.

Inevitability - Karma

I often use a pendulum as a gauge as to what I have cleared so far and as a guide to which area is holding the troubled energy. Do not get stuck looking for accurate answers from it. The beginning is to assume there is clearing needed in any area you alight on. Therefore, you can start it swinging and get the healing work underway. As the pendulum slows, start it again with the intention to clear more. Gradually it will settle quicker and you will know you are coming to the end of the turbulence.

So the next inevitability is karma. Whether you believe in it or have never given it any thought, it is worth clearing it. You will have witnessed suffering disproportionate to one or another. In your own life, you will have experienced recurring themes in relationships and finances and health. Because difficulties happen time and again, most people doubt that real change is possible. If you do not clear your karma then change really is not possible. You are going to be forever paying karmic debts. This is experienced as an excessive amount of suffering. In addition, you will find yourself playing out karmic roles. These are experienced as regular dramas that may have different characters and different story lines but will have suspiciously similar outcomes!

Freeing yourself of karma using this process of bringing the light of awareness to it, allows you to transmute it. This is neither transcending it nor enduring it. It is consciously acknowledging it, at an energetic level. It releases the old knots of energy back into its fluid, unruffled state. From here it can take shape again as a life form or a lit bit of pure oxygen. It is all energy melding, forming and being expressed. This conscious acknowledgement is the cornerstone of energy clearing. It is the opportunity to bring chaos, wherever you see it, back to coherence. As you observe the energetic disturbance, you disperse it and your intention harmonizes more and more aspects of your life and anything else you decide to pay attention to. It presents an accelerated path to empowerment by addressing situations and observations directly. While your life is guided by inevitability in the form of karmic patterns, we are completely disempowered. You are on a treadmill, however hard you try to break new ground or hope for a turnaround.

Karma often shows up in your legs. Hip and knee pain and joint replacements indicate a symbolic difficulty in moving forward in life. This, in turn, alerts you to the inexplicable deterioration, that is stopping you in your tracks. The considerable pain in the limbs and the emotional desperation at not being able to do what you love to do, are typical of karmic suffering. Examples of karma readily unravelled are a bank manager who's ankles had given way and put paid to his one joy which had been golf; a dancer who could not spin or turn due to a mystery knee pain; three pianists, all of whom could no longer play. One due to performance anxiety, one from repetitive strain injury and one with arthritis. All the problems had a karmic source.

Identify the source - this is simply an energy field where a problem took root, rather than identifying a whole story about 'why' you accrued a trouble - and then shake out the traces and associated disturbance in your other energy fields. For example, karma might be the root, then fear and frustration in the mental energy field, then conflict in the home as the physical manifestation. As quickly as you can allow it, energy is released and harmonious movement happens. Positive thinking does have its place as you must constantly remember that it is an energetic universe and therefore fluid and reparable, rather than solid and damaged. Also you must be prepared to put good attitudes in place of the old beliefs you are giving up. Initially, the clearing of inevitability is freeing your mind. Even if you are skeptical of terms like karma or divination, or beliefs, or the unconscious mind, still clear them. You also do not know where electricity comes from or the ingredients in a pain killer but you still use it. That is what you should do now. Just give each one of those terms five minutes clearing. You lose nothing and gain, at very least, an interesting experiment and insight into who you are and what you feel strongly about. This is a step into objectivity, which will lead to detachment from all sorts of drama in itself.

The outline of this empowerment process is to clear the turbulence in yourself. Then regularly remember the interconnectedness of all life because this halts the illusion that we are all separate. It reminds us that, more fundamental than all our categories and understandings, there is an energetic fabric, fluid and untroubled. Once clarity is achieved, you must stop identifying with difficulties in your environment. You will notice toxicity and be sensitive to people but these frequencies will then be recognized and let go, on contact, rather than triggering painful spirals to your own heart. In the end, you will have developed the greatest gift of all; the ability to direct your thoughts constructively and consciously create your own reality. You will be telling a different story about the world: The friendships you have appreciated, the resources you have had, the health you and your family have enjoyed and the adventures life has taken you on. With your focus firmly on well being and gratitude, you will watch with a lifting heart how your outer reality starts to reflect these new feelings, ten fold. As you are always participating in creating your current reality, start healing right away, to ensure conscious participation from now on. As you allow both this understanding of an energetic reality and how to energetically heal yourself, to sink in, you will inadvertently be uploading the two things you need; the release of a limited view and the ability to interact with the whole energetic field. Instead of inexorable perseverance, you get to live your life as a deliberate creation.

Inevitability - Entity Attachments
The next form of inevitability that you are up against are entity attachments. These can take three main forms; memories of difficult people you have known, negative thought forms and unconscious beliefs. Attachments are like dents in your energetic armour. At the slightest hint of something similar in your present moment, like a facial expression, a turn of phrase or even a jacket, you are triggered in to a reaction to a memory. You might think that you take people as you find them and are not judgmental, but this is deeper. The old association makes a fresh perspective impossible.

If you clear your entity attachments, you are acknowledging the original memory. Have compassion for yourself, not berating yourself with too much harsh 'get over it' in your attitude. Bear in mind, it might not even be your memory or it may have happened to you, but when you were only a child and could not make sense of it. With compassion though, I do ask you to get over it too. Do not let yourself get lost in a bad memory and justify the toll it has taken on your life. You do not want to get to the pearly gates still going on about something that happened years ago. Letting things go is going to take practice but now is the time to start. You clear the emotional charge around your darkest thoughts, when you clear your entity attachments. Then you are in a position to clear the traces you have carved out to them since. Bitterness, shame spirals, anger and hurt are such traces; all of them increasingly toxic if not released. I recommend using a pendulum to clear the majority. You can start it swinging and as it starts to slow, ask again if there are more to clear. Most people I have worked with have had thousands but, this way, they only take a matter of minutes to clear.

There will be some obvious attachments that you are aware of anyway, like your parents, teachers and countless other more dubious characters. One way to release their hold over your mood and health is to say the old mantra 'I love you, I'm sorry, forgive me and thank you'. You will notice huge resistance when you first say it, especially if it is to someone who has abused you in any way. You will know you have healed it when you no longer mind. Holding a grudge and not forgiving is, as they say, like buying a vial of poison for vengeance and deciding to take it all yourself.

Another way to address people and entrenched beliefs is to see them as unloved parts of yourself. Everything is just a reflection of a part of you that needs healing. You can count yourself lucky when you are the harmless one, rather than the perpetrator. In this sense, it is appropriate to thank them, as you made them behave badly to bring up something you need to heal. If your mind complains and thinks of examples of innocent victims of crimes and tragedy, just ignore it for now. Your job is to bring yourself back in to balance. What we are doing for the moment is letting go of the dramatic, traumatic and painful memories you have stored, so you yourself do not keep getting lost in the darkness, following old trains of thought down blind alleys and cul de sacs.

Inevitability - Alienation

In an energetic universe, one can understand a person as one reflection of a many-sided mirror ball., reflecting back whatever it can see perfectly. Within the fluid fabric of energy, you can also understand yourself as being just a schism of energy. Over time, you identify with more and more around you. You see yourself as a man or woman, who is good at this and that, poor at this and that, has this and that etc. Quickly you give yourself a very small identity and a small place in the world, completely convinced that you see all there is to see. You have actually only succeeded in collecting a lot of very dense and conflicting energy around your original schism and called it 'Me'. Most people live unaware and devoid of their connection to the whole. Even more limiting is that most people have identified completely with their physical energy field. Not in a wild, experiential way but often stuck on the question of whether one is successful or attractive. I can confirm, you are attractive beyond measure; physically, mentally, emotionally, spiritually and in every other way. Your concern should be what exactly are you attracting and what are you shutting off. Until you have cleared the residue of karma and arbitrary attachments, you can only attract a demoralizingly repetitive array of people and episodes. Every living thing has been incarnated, in form, for a reason.

However, people must remember the magnitude of who they are before they can properly serve any purpose.

The third chronic sense of inevitability is, therefore, our alienation. From a very young age we are told that we are separate. We have individual needs for nourishment, affection, rest and education. We start to wonder if we are going to get enough and if there is enough to go around. We develop a sense of sharing a limited supply. This later becomes a 'lack mentality' affecting all areas of life. Most fundamentally, people quickly come to 'know' that everything is external and beyond their control. People have no trust whatsoever that there is a web of life sustaining them. They feel small and ineffective. Even if a person achieves individual power it is transient and uncertain. The power that we only have to remember is our connection to the whole. That means we can call on the energy of any deity, wild animal, ocean or genius, living or dead. It means we can heal any illness. It means we can come to trust ourselves and our ideas completely. The energy of persevering, individual ego stands down and you start to conduct a spiritual orchestra, capable of every sound and composition.

We can only notice our elaborate sense of alienation, one occasion at a time and start to play with alternative ideas. For example, your dog may be very unwell one morning and at first think 'Help! I need a vet to 'tell' me what's wrong. I need someone else to 'do' something. Let it occur to you that you are handing over your power, as soon as you go into fear. Try the idea 'What if ...we are all one and this animal is just an unloved part of the self needing attention. Settle down and clear all the energy fields and attachments you can think of. The malady was not there earlier and all may well be quiet and well again in an hour. Being in pain or seeing someone in pain are occasions when the majority of people suddenly believe they are separate and become in a hurry to hand over their power. Authority is another, security is another, money is another. These are all deeply entrenched divisions but you will notice that in nearly every relationship, personal or formal, there is little sense of us all being connected, let alone one.

A blanket clearing you can do is to pivot all alienated frequencies you have to ones of connection. You are disciplining yourself mentally too. Firstly, you are spending definite moments in your day, remembering you are part of everything there is. The relief on your mental and physical body will be great. After a while it will start to occur to you, as an uninvited thought, 'What if we are all one and this situation is just bringing a healing for me?' Before you know it, the understanding will be established firmly and you will be enjoying peace, inspired resolutions and comfortably taking responsibility for all your experience. Then you can play with uploading different parts of the spectrum of oneness, that you had not previously thought of. This might be the energy of Richard Branson to expand your entrepreneurial effectiveness or the agility of a snow leopard before a dance performance or the protection of the angels before a long drive home, in bad weather. Everything is accessible and an intrinsic part of you, you need no longer only identify with your physical condition and your Curriculum Vitae to date. Branch out!

Inevitability - Blame

The reason that most people do not heal is blame. They need their pain to be someone else's fault. As soon as you blame anyone for anything, you externalize and give away the chance you have. The chance we always have can be understood as constant opportunities to forgive. The pattern we have to practice is seeing every situation and person we meet as having shown up to let us heal a specific negative pattern. For example, you find yourself observing 'Oh, there is that anger again. I must give myself a moment to acknowledge that and let it go'. Previously you might have said 'That really makes me angry'. The differences between these two reactions are that, in the former, you have a moment of awareness of your feelings rather than getting lost in the details of the 3D drama that seemed to cause it. Secondly, you can witness and dispel endless hurt illusions each time, which means you do not have to create the same scenario again having not learnt the first five thousand times! For example, you might see, in your moment of awareness of anger, or in the acknowledgement you give it later, hurt illusions such as 'No one respects me', 'People are so ignorant', 'I was stupid to trust' and 'I hate that'. Remember that these are just unhelpful ideas you hold that are reverberating away in your unconscious all of the time, attracting confirmation and evidence that they are true. Ask that you can let them go from now on. It will be easier each time as your self acknowledgement in the moment has released the emotional charge, at last.

Direct your thoughts to the realization that there are all kinds of people and people can only respect you as far as you can respect yourself. Also remind yourself that people are not all ignorant, millions of people care deeply about each other. Remember that trust is the neural pathway down which any sort of relaxation and joy can travel, so it should be cultivated and sustained. Then, evidence in the form of trustworthy characters and fortuitous events can turn up. Also decide that hate is a toxicity that you determine not to give any more energy too. You are consciously shifting your perspective. It is partly mental work, applying this paradigm of an energetic universe in which we can participate as we choose and it is partly opening the generosity of your heart as it is less and less tied in knots of unacknowledged pain. You will

17

encounter many who are too hurt to care about themselves or anyone else. Often it is the insight that you are always your own worst enemy that brings the momentum to try. Loosen your attachment to old blame tactics and adopt positive mental attitudes.

Inevitability - Grief

Some say the reason they feel so bad is grief. Their childhood or someone's close to them was snatched away. The reasoning is, you must not let the pain go away, or who will hold the memory? Also, the events were so humbling, so desperate that they will always define your life. Explaining to St Peter, at the pearly gates, that you never did anything or loved anyone etc because you were completely occupied with grief is not the way to go. Take a moment now to clear 'grieving someone's absence' down to 0% and 'celebrating your presence' up to 100%. To make sure it is complete, the pendulum is a good gauge. Start it swinging and, as it slows, start it for the next ten percent until you are there. A pendulum is as easy to come by as a strand of string and a curtain ring. Anything at all will do. A little bit of weight helps though, when you start, to get a clarity of movement.

Any resistance you feel to 'celebrating your own presence' is important to notice too. Most people do not think much of themselves, on the quiet. You might not know what exactly is wrong with you and be consistently trying your best but, nonetheless, you suspect you are getting something wrong or you would be more sure of yourself. Furthermore, the idea of loving, looking after and investing in yourself can sound absurd and feel uncomfortable at first. I guarantee that the more positive emotion you pour into your life and actions though, the more successful your future creations will be.

If you are missing someone, you can clear them too. For example you can forgive them for their absence and forgive yourself too. This is extremely helpful, whether the departure was chosen, as in a separation, or final, as in dying. It is useful to remember that we are only twenty percent physical. This means any conscious attention you pay to someone will be greatly appreciated and at least 80% effective. In the case of someone who has died you can 'send them to the light', 'clear any trauma before and at the time of death', 'heal your own relationship to the person' and ask if there is 'any lesson or wisdom they would like you to hear'. This might be delivered in a dream or via someone you find yourself talking to. Bear in mind that, when you clear, you are not dismissing a memory, you are just recognizing and healing the emotional turbulence around the memory. This is good for everyone involved, as stuck energy is released and, in some cases the soul.

No person who has passed on wants vengeance for anything or for you to remain sorry for them or yourself. Thankfully, no dead person even wishes to still be alive. You can communicate with all the friends you have lost over the years. You will find that they are willing and keen to offer trustworthy guidance, now they have left this world of attachment. If we believe that a person has completely gone, they can neither interact any further with this plane or successfully move on. Work on releasing recalcitrant pain and expanding your understanding of what is happening, for friends present and absent.

Chapter Three

A Way Forward - Your Soul

Living physically in chaos and reactivity, we need a bridge into our true nature. Once you have cleared the flotsam and jetsam of obstacles in the way, use the divining method to develop a bridge of intuition. By clearing, you allow for moments of awareness, where you would have been triggered in the past. Instead of being instantly driven to hurt, anger or fear, you find you can consciously invite in more of the energetic spectrum. Choose to invite in any positive concepts you have recognized in the past. For example, the 'infinite organizing power of nature', the 'power of God', the 'navigational skill of the fox', the 'faithfulness of the dog', the 'clarity of angels', the 'wisdom of your ancient self' that has been incarnated countless times before and the 'gaiety of your child self', the 'fearlessness of a bear' and your 'connection to the highest good' etc. Because of your new understanding of the interconnected nature of life, you find you can dip into this pot of all that there is and make a new set of associations.

Visually, you can imagine snipping the chords of needs and wants and consciously choosing new guides. Soon, these spiritual frequencies - navigational skill, faithfulness, clarity, wisdom, fearlessness and connection can become your established motivations to action. You will not need the pendulum to ascertain the course to take, unless you are feeling ungrounded or upset. Very soon, you will have the great gift of self trust. It is a great relief on your own system. This is because, until now, decisions will have been revisited, emotionally, many times. Sometimes with the same judgement, sometimes with regret or anxiety. From here on in you can stand by your decisions with conviction.

A Way Forward - Energetic Implications

When you start to see everything as energy condensed into many forms, no one thing is terribly serious, nothing is even good or bad. A long-standing sickness and a common cold are separated only by the person's attachment to the piece of energetic information arising. Therefore, it can be treated in exactly the same way, by clearing the attachment. All you have to acknowledge each time is that you are, inadvertently, holding a frequency and resonating it so strongly that it has taken shape in your body. As you become aware of it, there is no need to go into 1. fear or 2. resignation to your fate or 3. denial. These three habitual approaches compound the information, embedding it further in the physical body. Even if the source of the illness is something in the environment or something so-called 'infectious' or 'genetic', clearing your relationship to the emerging information will release it. You will not have to embody it fully and keel over, or whatever the usual prognosis.

What is happening in your energetic fields when you 'release attachment to' something is that you are reminding yourself that everything is part of this oceanic mass of energy. Any problems you meet are just things that you have previously given too much attention to. You have always been picking and choosing what aspects of oneness to identify with. Furthermore, you have then been holding on to them as if they are true or fighting them because they are depressing you. So, releasing is noticing what you have created, without judgement. This compassionate assessment aligns the information and increases self acceptance. This allows your parameters to soften and activates a fearless curiosity about the whole great field of potential to explore.

Up until now, choices were unconscious, often primed by your upbringing. Then they were condensed into your current reality, within which you settled or at least settled for. The more aware you become, the more conflict and resistance fall away. Large tracts of chaotic and emotionally charged information are neutralized and you are starting to heal. At the beginning of our lives, we did not have this strong sense of individuation. Your mother and father and everything else within reach were felt to be a part of us. As an adult, however, it will take some effort to remember this feeling of belonging. Gradually, you will spend more and more of each day feeling connected again. Your awareness of your energetic, rather than merely physical, participation in life becomes a focus. You are establishing a way of being that is fluid, healthy and expansive.

An inner certainty that you can direct your thoughts and fully commit yourself to what you want, without sabotaging it, is empowering. Hot on its heels, though, is the responsibility to create something beneficial. Thankfully, once your deep sense of inevitability has gone and you no longer identify with the memories that hindered you, it is possible to hear and apply your very own guidance system. This will be some of the time to start with but then all the time. This extra dimension is well able to coordinate your desires with what you already have happening in your current reality. Success is no longer seen as something selfish, that involves receiving the cherry on the cake at others' expense. Quite the opposite, success is realizing more and more who you truly are and making the most of it. A great amount of people focusing on the abundance and potential of our energetic world increases the energy flowing to everyone's efforts. The job becomes to get clarity about what you do want. This is more difficult than it sounds. Ask yourself now to outline five things things you truly desire. I guarantee that your mind will travel first, or at least quickly, to what you do not want. Next you will, hopefully, be able to drum up some more positive statements, no doubt followed, though, by the 'buts' and 'only ifs' of qualifying statements. If you give this positive mental framing work some attention, eventually you will get a coherent vision. Only then, can it start taking shape. The implicit warning here is that negative thinking is addictive and positive thinking is not. Do not consider this exercise frivolous and miss yet another opportunity to create something worthwhile.

A Way Forward - Balance As A Complete Vision
One answer on the list of what most people want is a balance in their lives. We have seen that one moves closer to achieving a goal, the more clarity one has about it. To this end, we can focus, in a methodical way, on what balance might mean in each energy field.

The physical energy field. Physical Balance can be understood as keeping your centre of gravity. Feel if you lean equal weight on both feet. Experiment with your posture, lifting your sternum, bringing your shoulder blades down. Increase your balance on one leg, on your arms or just shoulders. Anyone can improve their physical balance with practice, from whatever their current condition.

The spiritual energy field. The two sides of the body should also be balanced energetically. Using the pendulum, clear for equal softness versus tension in the muscle tone of your left and right sides. Just bringing your attention to it, becoming aware of how your body feels from the inside, will also isolate and correct the balance. It is generally thought that your right side represents your male side and your left represents your female side. If you reflect on which side of your body you have aches and pains, a frozen shoulder, ankles that give way and so on, this offers further healing insight.

The mental energy field. Your thoughts might turn to 'Well, that explains it, its a lost cause' or 'I never could touch my toes anyway'. Notice these limiting beliefs. In the past, they may have stopped you making improvements. This time, clear your attachment to the beliefs as you become aware of them. Take an objective role. No longer identifying with the idea that you are a solid, sightly rickety, physical being. You are, in fact, the awareness behind the thoughts. Perhaps using the pendulum, swing it until you get your resistant thoughts from 100 to 0%, then upload a better attitude up to 100%. For example, 'I am grateful for what I am able to do' and 'I am enjoying how balanced I'm becoming'. What you will notice is that the universe conspires to bring you to the new mental vision of yourself.

People pray for peace of mind but you can start by embodying it, physically. Every person is animated. Your physical presence is characterized by aspects of your mental personality. Instead of trying to quiet the mind or relax as you used to, it is worth bypassing the mind altogether. Focus on the core of your body and emanate tenderness outwards. This is from the centre of the fingers, toes and limbs, to the skin on the surface. Inform every cell to represent this comfort and ease. Hold the same intention for your shoulders and chest. When you literally choose the frequencies you want to embody, you find that at once they bring health. This is conscious choice at its best. Repeated practice brings a new way of being in the world. A focus on the light rather than the darkness, on the vitality and animation of the body rather than the individual aches and pains. New slip streams of fitness and self expression present themselves.

The emotional field. Emotional balance is achieved by developing your sense of belonging. If you immediately look outside for evidence and decide 'No, I am very much on my own in this', 'People don't understand me' or 'There is no real community anymore', just notice these ideas coming up. The solution is, again, to look inwards, to our remembered knowledge that we are all connected and take comfort from that. It is balancing to remember our oneness in other ways too; that love underlies every situation and that there is nothing to judge as we are all innocent reflections of each other. There will be clearing to do regularly over this because our distrust is so ingrained. We have drifted a long way off the mark, with our perceptions, because we were so convinced of our separateness. Over time, your intuitive knowing will go from being a guide you check in with occasionally, to being an ongoing sense that you are powerfully participating in a great healing for yourself and all mankind.

In our other energetic fields, too, there is profound information coming to help keep our balance. Sometimes it is in our etheric field, from our environment. If you can remain receptive and centred in your awareness, a sustainable expansion is happening. Try and picture yourself dispersing the emotional and electrical charge around your most dominant and recurring feelings. Practice witnessing all your daily interactions as gifts, however tense or unexpected. If you can continually drag your mind away from blame and judgement, you open up the range of experience to include health where there was sickness, curiosity where there was fear and leadership where there were only victims of circumstance. You find yourself balanced, philosophical and with your physical batteries recharged simultaneously.

A Way Forward - The Energy Clearing Process

Even when you have cleared old depressing attachments and inevitability in all its guises, it will not become your second nature to automatically make positive changes. Unfortunately, the very events that closed your heart down, in the first place, will come up for healing. Be prepared for this and clear a little every day of your vast memory bank of experiences. This can be done by simply starting the day by clearing any obstacles to this being the best day of your life so far. Then, ending the day by clearing any difficult information that you met or absorbed during the day. By catching yourself at these, least emotional, times you can get a glimpse of objectivity. Instead of your mind saying 'Oh really' or 'I don't think so!', you are setting an optimistic tone. In the morning, you are aligning your thoughts to help you make steady, positive progress throughout your day. In the evening, you are directing them towards a calm and compassionate review of your day. The acknowledgment releases the stress of the drama your day may have contained.

You can use the words drama, polarity, turbulence, disease, chaos, stress, conflict and story interchangeably. In our energetic world they are all just expressions. They all represent tangles and vortices of energy, too dense or draining away, respectively. To heal anything only involves remembering this. As you start to feel the benefit of your morning and evening clearings, start to call upon this energetic perspective to deal with other situations. 'Can I clear my relationship with my parents? Can I clear the bad luck my friend always has? Can I clear the atmosphere at work? That disease that is killing off the Dutch Elms? That pain that is making my partner's life desperate?' Every difficulty is something either in you or your environment that is showing up for healing. On the surface there seems to be something wrong, but you are training your focus to return to the coherent flow that underlies it. Therefore, you can use the words stillness, harmony, perfection, oneness, all that is, oceanic flow and energetic fabric interchangeably as well. We are establishing a pattern of living in alignment with this.

A Way Forward - Non judgement

What stands as a barrier between you and this peaceful existence is judgement. As you embark on participating consciously, you will start to notice what you feel strongly about. You will have thought you were absolutely right about several things, like being anti- cruelty to animals, neglect of children, nuclear power, domestic abuse. You might be pro- organic food, good education for all, multi cultural inclusion and marriage. In fact, nothing is good or bad. It is actually people getting triggered by strong emotion to various topics that perpetuates problems. Righteous indignation and an overactive critical faculty are the main culprits in academic and scientific people. Low self esteem and a lack mentality are the main culprits for others. Polarized, black and white thinking is everywhere though. Common, to all instances, is the denial of our interconnectedness. Your job is to dissipate these embedded ideas as you notice them.

The ethical implications are that everyone is innocent. Some people have just identified with different things. You might have been careful to only express your sunny disposition or your tough-but-fair attitude. Someone else might have learnt to scowl at the world to make sure they got what they needed. Fundamentally, every person has all the frequencies to play with. As you get comfortable with more and more thoughts and feelings of your own and those of whoever shows up, your inner world will expand. The way to practice this is to keep remembering it. It is an affirmation that most people will have to have play with first before in anyway believing it, understanding it or trusting it! So have fun with statements like 'I am going to assume that this happened because of an innocent misunderstanding!' The truth of this statement will unfold. In the past, you would have felt anger at the cause of the trouble. You might have been defensive, cautious of more negativity to come. Throughout, you would have been implying your doubt about a positive outcome. Therefore, you were inadvertently guaranteeing there would not be one.

Play continually with the awareness that each scenario and person you meet, you have created yourself. Firstly, this stops old blame patterns. You become much more inclined to understand events and reach a harmonious solution. After a while, you establish an expansive process where you recognize every situation as an opportunity to meet yourself, know yourself, come to terms with yourself. Many people spend so long in crisis that their resistance to taking responsibility for their life is too great. They are literally dying to hand their lives over to science to experiment on...and then be angry at the results! Instead, please assume there is simply some stuck energy to clear, some residue from the past and make the transition to the new paradigm as soon as you feel ready.

Chapter Four
Structure supporting the new paradigm

All architects learn about sacred geometry and the golden mean but many do not use it in their designs. The golden mean is 1.618, which appears uniformly in all living things. It is the ratio between one part and the next; torso to legs, wings to thorax, leaf to twig. Growth and health resonate most successfully at this frequency, that is why it is mirrored everywhere. It should be applied in man-made constructions, in particular homes and work premisses, for families and businesses to thrive. It is also the only way that buildings can really benefit their environment, rather than pollute it. The golden mean is illustrated by a spiral, which is the most common form found in nature, from snails to DNA to whole galaxies.

We have accepted that we live in an energetic world. Everything we see and experience is energy compressed in to various forms, some tangible some not. Emotion is a cascade between short and long wave frequencies. This can be understood as immediate feelings given momentum by memories from your past. Imagine if you could consciously move every feeling along a spiral, to its resolution. The geometry, in addition to the heart space that you are becoming aware of, can provide this instant resolution and healing. You are consciously reconnecting to the central still point that underlies all apparent suffering. The spiral offers a perfectly manageable path to follow, through denial, avoidance, pain or panic back to your peaceful core.

Sacred geometry is also concerned with successful manifesting. We can understand how it assists in bringing thought in to form. The spiral is the only geometry that allows energy and information to fall in to its centre. As energy gets compressed, it goes the speed of light and therefore comes to inhabit time. It becomes manifest. Have a golden spiral at your centre, whether it is a piece of art, or a spiral staircase, and make it a creative space to set out your goals. They then cannot help but take shape in the third dimension.

Understanding that you have your own geometric structure corrects your health as well. In a human being there is a build up of electrical charge and emotional charge. Feelings and experiences eventually take shape in the body as disease. We are stuck with a compelling illusion that we are separate from everyone else and we spend our time trying to fend off the pressure from this 'outside world'. We fear judgement, pain, violence, destitution and other apparent derelictions. Unfortunately, that means we keep attracting them because the fear is continually there in our unconscious.

Furthermore, most people think they are solid, limited and, what is worse, they are sure they are deteriorating. People have altogether forgotten that energy is flowing from and to them all the time, changing our very composition. We are not solid but fluid, energetic beings made up mostly of light and space and water. Conscious use of the spiral cannot help but create a spin path for all these conflicting and demoralizing bits of energetic information that have been identified with. With the release of this stagnant information, stress in the physical system also falls away.

Geometry can bring about effortless positive change. Although it is unchanging itself, it facilitates the forming and dissipation of energy. Remember that you have only adopted an idea of who you are and then become it. You can now change very simply by changing your ideas and bringing them into form, becoming something else instead. Limit yourself, if you want, to conventional healing methods but realize that you are swallowing inevitability and fear as a way of life. Or you might allow stilted progress along a very linear path at most. Change is possible on every level. Emotional, mental, physical, spiritual and in your environment. Do not assume that all is lost in regard to love, time, health or even money, however long you have been ill or despairing.

Your awareness will consciously raise more and more old beliefs, damage and resistance that have been stored inside you. Resistance is futile. All you have to practice is seeing all of life as an opportunity rather than a challenge, learning to let go and become powerful. Do not horde all those bleak moments as if they are what makes you you. In geometric terms, a human being is a linear projected force but the spiral geometry creates a non linear spin path, where there is no resistance. If you utilize the geometry, even while doodling at work, you are sweeping your nervous system in towards a central stillness. Infinite compression is possible of apparent conflicts like right and wrong, sick or well and positive and negative. Imagine your life with no internal conflicts. As your mind alights upon this wonderful prospect, perhaps clear them too now, to assist their resolution. You might find you have hundreds. Nonetheless, do not add a story, analysis or justification, just ask to let them go ten at a time. The sigh of relief will be far reaching.

The heart of the spiral in healing is a still point of focused awareness and compassion. You can maximize the velocity of the spin path and multiply its results. In personal terms, a wish or a thought is the centering force in your body and surroundings. Therefore, you increase your power via conscious intentions. If your thoughts are not based on love, they produce a toxic centre or no centre at all. On one hand, this is fortunate as it renders someone without integrity less powerful, rather than powerful to negative effect! Coherence and clarity are the most successful creative force. On the other hand though, you will realize how few of your daily thoughts about your self, life and other people are based on love? As you start to notice the level of magnetism you wield, for both good and bad, you will take on the work more and more readily. The task is to commit to a compassionate understanding of yourself and others. That is the still point that this geometry and healing work establishes in you. A clear heart then makes us available to be of service. On a micro level, the heart allows infinite cycles to nest together and maintain health in a person. The infinity of cycles are also spreading the healing exponentially, from you to others, to the whole of reality.

Beneath the world of things we can see, lies a structure of light. This can be imagined as a hologram and the beams are held in place by their geometric arrangement. Everything we see exists in this form too. For healing, you can return anything to its fundamental frequency of structural integrity. Even a painting of a spiral or an ornament or visualization actively draws the person, who observes it, back towards their own structural integrity. The relationship is one of sympathetic resonance. This is something like empathizing, feeling for someone and wishing them well.

The ventricles of a human heart also operate in a simple spiral movement. We can see how the heart-to-heart energy clearing work amplifies the sympathetic resonance and magnifies the power of the call back to health. It is because our hearts are, at once, in spiral form but also conscious, active, intentional and compassionate. The energy cannot resist shifting. The heart directs it and the body responds and releases the stress. Physical change occurs and it marks a true return to form. For people who are working towards empowerment, conscious choice and participation, sacred geometry is therefore very useful in your environment. Do not get sidetracked by fear that you will take on other people's difficulties. That is an unconscious habit. With consciousness, you are creating a space between you and the other person, wherein turbulence is calmed. The horizons of the two hearts overlap and what each has learnt is acknowledged. The other reason not to get stuck on questions like how to protect yourself is that, even asking the very question, means you have forgotten the point again. You have, by mistake, returned to the judgement that there is good and bad energy. You have returned to the assumption that you are separate and vulnerable. You have returned to the conclusion that problems are real and personal. All these ideas perpetuate rather than heal.

Chapter Five

Presence

The Importance Of Being Present

Joy is the highest energy of all. You can only feel joy to the extent that you can live in the present moment, untroubled by multiple considerations. The main reason people are not present is that there is something sad in their heart that they cannot face and let go of. Everyone knows someone who cannot hold eye contact. Everyone has themselves felt uncomfortable meeting the eyes of someone when a difficult issue is being discussed. What is happening, in that moment, is that we are being triggered into the past, may be with anger or the future, say by fear. As you clear the old bad feeling that has hung around for decades, you have a chance to stay open minded, open hearted and listening whatever is happening, rather than being emotionally derailed onto an old piece of dead end track. Rather than avoid discomfort, decide to face it with interest. For this to help you move on, rather than be a self torture, you have to practice a gentle process. This can be described as continually forgiving yourself and anyone else for their reactions.

Becoming Present

The Process: Forgiveness

Try and think of forgiveness as an exercise. The more you depersonalize the mission, the better. Many have a very short mental process when the word forgiveness is mentioned. To generalize, the thoughts of those that need forgiveness go straight to justifications for their actions and the thoughts of those who need to forgive go straight to examples of things that are unforgivable! Draw an example of each situation from your own past. You might have behaved badly and hurt someone. In your mind, see them and apologize. Ask for their forgiveness. Energetically this sets them free as it sets you free. Then forgive yourself. Regret and guilt are the lowest energies around. They subdue every function of the body.

Forgiveness is the only way to release negative emotion and move on in any sort of a powerful way. Even if your mind tells you that you have nothing to be ashamed of, you will notice you do still feel bad. So start letting those low vibrations go. Even if you are not sure whether to blame yourself or problems with another, it does not matter. If, like everyone else, you have been sure for a very long time that you are separate and other people are unjust and abusive etc, you will be carrying around some of this negative emotion. Frustration, resentment and anger are similar forms of un-forgiveness to guilt and regret. They are all toxic and paralyzing. Start with quite insignificant events from your past that do not have too much emotional charge around them and then acknowledge higher impact events. The motivation is that you do not wish to continue to suffer. If you resist this practice on the grounds of righteousness, clear that first.

The Means: A Compassionate Heart

Being aware should be a very subtle process. Do not bulldoze your emotions by insisting on non attachment to anybody or any thing. Do not berate yourself with relentless judgement of your past and your current life situation. Subtlety is required to start noticing the life beneath your life situation. It is the gentle pulse of your heart responding to information. Your heart can acknowledge things on many levels. First the emotional heart experiences hurt and hostility, warmth and empathy and everything in between. Underneath this, you can access the clearing heart. In this context, the heart is understood as a proactive tool, capable of spreading light on any darkness and healing any amount of turbulence through its infinite capacity for resonance. It can be visualized as a flotation tank, within which we can return any troubled energy to true form. Thirdly, there is our ancient heart. There is a sense in which we have all been here and done this before. We are not a mere few decades old, we are timeless. Whatever drama and dilemmas we meet, we have seen them all before. One could sum the three up as our senses, unconditional love and wisdom. All these aspects of our hearts require us to listen and accept what we hear, not brutally face the music and whip ourselves in to shape! It is often said that we should take our attention away from the external signs of who we are and how we are doing. Put time aside to remember your heart and let its many dimensions lead your attention within.

Perhaps you have written off this crucial facet, your heart, as broken, lost or less accurate than your brain? I'll deal with the broken heart first. The problem with a broken heart is that it is love and grief tied in a very big knot. One minute you think you are tugging loose a strand of grief and ready to move onwards and upwards, only to find you have tightened the hold of your heart strings. The tension leads to breaking point. It does not take much. Someone can unexpectedly show you a small kindness and you find yourself in a heap. You can have just taken a shine to someone only to jump to the feeling of having been used. More often, you shut down and privately vow never to feel anything at all again. This level of bad feeling can carry through generations as cellular memory and manifests again and again as heart attacks and cancer. So it is fairly important to heal your heart. This can be done simply by acknowledging what is stored there.

The heart is a tetrahedral-shaped muscle and as such can hold millions upon millions of bits of information and frequencies, without them conflicting. The way people have it set up emotionally though is like a love heart-shaped room with one or two incongruous pieces of furniture in it, that must be avoided or run into. Picture a suite consisting of a three seater sofa of guilt, an armchair of sadness and another armchair of some unfamiliar but toxic-looking material. The result is that no hopeful feeling can get past and no tentative idea can receive your full investment. Once you have the realization that your heart can handle anything, being open and receptive, you know everything you need to know. The emotional charge that surrounded your worst memories and fears starts to disperse. The shock leaves the rest of your body too, leaving you less reactive and more able to respond instead. Your heart returns to its harmonious flow of information in and out. You will be able to experience the whole spectrum of feelings from creative and blissful through to angry or painful without judging any of them as good or bad. Best of all though, you will be able to freely express your love again.

The Lost Heart. Nobody actually loses their heart. Strangely, people quickly give their feelings of power and joy away but hold on tight to their negative experiences. You might be surprised to hear how hopeless people are at letting anything go. Some people say 'Well yes, I've forgiven but I'll never forget'. Others say, 'Oh, I hardly ever think of it but it was definitely quite damaging at the time'. Off they go, etching it deeper into their hearts. People with a noble cause are even more tenacious. This may be in support of an underdog or it may be because they have a strong ethical perspective but, nevertheless, people hang on to every grim detail, whether they are aware of it or not. If we look further afield, or at least in to one, we notice that trees know a thing or two about the rhythms and seasons of nature. They do not hold on to their leaves, they let them fall. Without fear or a shadow of a doubt, they demonstrate their trust that more leaves will grow.

We can practice letting go of the things we are emotionally attached to. This works best as a systematic exercise, lining up many people or things, each time, in your mind's eye and clearing the feelings that arise. Simply deciding to let go of your attachment to your partner or children for ten minutes allows a healthy breathing space. This is because relationships are often obscured by dynamics of guilt, anxiety and responsibility. We are supposed to enjoy ourselves and each other. For this to happen, it is really beneficial to let go of years of conditioning as well, again just by consciously choosing to. Incidentally, the tao understanding of making love is that it should have nine courses, with all sorts of rapture and ending in the woman's complete letting go, into bliss. The man's role in this being one of butler, glad to be of service, perhaps! The other main reason to remember to let things go, as soon as they happen, is because bitterness and resentment will follow otherwise and probably end in an ulcer.

Until you learn to release this emotional charge, around your good and bad experiences equally, your inner life will remain very polarized. You might achieve super positivity but alternate it with periods of despondency. Or oscillate between peace and total resentment. All the above are states disconnected from oneness and therefore disempowering. Paradoxically, you can only connect to this one unified field by becoming aware that you are already participating in it. Your emotions, your intelligence, your body are all drawn from it. They are held together and called 'you' by a process of identification. You have chosen the current combination and now you must choose to identify and identify with a more expansive sense of self. For example, your soul's journey over many lifetimes; compassion for all living things; nature in all its magnificence; and the infinite. It is a paradox because one must see the sacred in oneself to realize that you are not an individual. The more elaborate the appreciation of who you are, the more the illusion of our alienation from each other falls away. We can continually dip in to the flow of all that is. Gamboling, frolicking, confidently diving and retrieving and recognizing yourself in everyone that you meet.

You must recognize your own spirit in order to recognize the spirit in anyone else. This is also why you can only experience love to the extent that you can show it to yourself. If you deep down loathe yourself, feel you do not deserve much and think you are missing a vital part that might make you human or lovable, then you might want to start exploring the question, what is love? If you are currently being abused around the clock by everyone you meet, again you are up against a twisted understanding of love. Love comes in many forms that all have their merits but, in short, it is a willingness to be present and pay attention.

As you cultivate a relationship with yourself you find out, gradually, what is holding you back. It may be painful or cringe worthy events. It may be fear. It is likely to be a multitude of mental and emotional experiences. Therefore, love is also the commitment to explore your own blocks and triggers as a welcome part of your inner landscape. In relationships, this translates into an ever expanding comfort zone of shared experience with your partner. Romantic love, projection of your hopes and dreams, needs, obsessions and intensity all get a lot of bad press but they all have their part to play in the grand theatre of our lives. However much you love someone and however much your family and work need physically, mentally and emotionally from you, a priority must be to maintain your internal connection to your infinite source.

The Obstacle: Stress

It is stress that drives us straight in to action. You will have noticed that most people are reactive rather than responsive. There should be an international plan implemented for stress management. Everyone is affected. Pessimism and anxiety are common place and are considered simply realistic. Furthermore, environmental stress travels under every surface and no one even guesstimates what is transmitted through our bodies from the operations of wireless systems. Electrical activity causes stress on the body, re-wiring our sensitive circuits to the stronger currents passing through. Geopathic stress lines in the ground emit toxic gases. Every stretch of land and city holds eons of history too. All these invisible but dense energies have been playing on your fragile nerves. Then you have your own life story to attach the stress to. It is equally valid, full of hardship, responsibility and uncertainty. Next thing you know, you have made the stress your own. Without realizing it, you own the stress fully and quite quickly it takes shape in your body in the form of high blood pressure, relationships breaking down or something else.

There are two parts to managing stress. One is becoming aware of it in your environment. The more you are conscious of, the less it is wearing you down on the quiet. You might end up running a mile from some places, looking for new work or spending every weekend by the sea but you will be aware and responding, rather than soldiering on. Secondly, choose not to identify with it or own it. Stress comes up, it is familiar but it is not who you are. It is one of many feelings that are around. Only acknowledge it and then put another thought and feeling in its place. Say to yourself 'This is not yours or mine, it just is.' Be determined in moving on and not drenching every cell of your body in the anxiety and adrenalin. There is a part of you that is peaceful and still, return there as often as you can.

How to be present for yourself
This particular moment is your best opportunity to be here, totally present and to be alive. There is no other moment. Life is an opportunity for a continual movement of regeneration. Keep recreating your linear reality with a more colourful and loving perspective. To spend this moment lamenting the past and worrying about the future guarantees more lamenting to be done. This is because the content of your thoughts is always creating your future. For the same reason, a sedentary approach of being 'past caring' leads to hopeless future creations as well.

To create the perfect now it is important to go inward to the soul to find clarity. This, by the way, is not the same as finding evidence that the world is a bad place and certainty that not a thing can be done about it! It is more a clarity consisting of a cleared inner landscape where old perspectives that were aligned with chaos and powerlessness take up none of your time. A vision, of what resolutions are possible, are what your mind alights upon. Your intentions then resonate from you in actions fueled by friendship, interest and inner knowing of our connectedness.

Presence as Happiness

Because we are all one and have chosen our experiences, it follows that happiness is our own concern. Unfortunately, what follows from that is the realization that you have been systematically depressing yourself all your life. It is time now to turn those dynamics around, into a way of being called happiness, for want of a better world - word, I mean! Your mission, if you should choose to accept it, is to treat yourself well. Initially, you will not be able to hear yourself clearly, from under the blanket of denial and avoidance where feelings have resided, shame-faced, since we were young. Peace and happiness grow, however, with a commitment to listen to what you have to say and to notice with compassion the areas clouded by low self esteem and guilt. Remember that, in every moment, you have the opportunity to make a new choice.

Presence as Fearlessness

It might be useful to do an inventory of what you are afraid of. This starts to get fears out in the daylight. As you grow up, you are not afraid of the dark so much. Or are you, except you now have a family or partner in the house to protect, or be protected by, so you do not think about it? Many emotional fears hold people in a lonely experience, for example fear of rejection and fear of loss. Then you notice your life is stuck in an apparent impasse. What is it that stops you from opening your mind to the infinite possibilities available to you? Again it is fear. It has sealed up your entire creative capacity, your resourcefulness, imagination and ability to express love. It is worth dealing with. First you have to know your fears and then you have to practice being okay with them. See yourself as flanked by love and power, whoever represents those strengths for you, and facing your fears. In such good company, you will find yourself addressing your fears from a firm but friendly perspective.

Fears only show up as an opportunity to learn something about yourself, do not miss the opportunity. When it comes to financial fear, I know there is a consensus. Everyone is agreed that we are in trouble. More important to remember, though, is that it is the collective fear that has created the problem. There was greed and there was desperation, both sides of the same scarce coin; fear of not having enough. If we hold the fear in ourselves we can only have it reflected back. Because we are all connected, we create it again and again. Practice feeling secure about money, make gratitude for what you do have become a familiar feeling. It will start as a mental exercise. The gift is to bring yourself back in to the present moment. Fear only exists as memory of past events or anxiety about the future. Do not forget that you belong here. You have access to everything you need and you are perfectly equipped for everything life brings. Technically, that is the only way it can be, in this intelligent, infinite, fluid energy field we live in.

Presence as Positive Change

It occurs to most people every day that they should try harder, if not be altogether different from how they are. The obvious downside to this thought process is that it repeatedly informs you that you are not alright as you are. Instead of being a motivating force behind self improvement, it is a passion killer of self criticism. However, if your self acceptance grows, you can fundamentally change the way you are. From overweight or underweight to a radiant expression of aliveness; from too old or too young to a warm respect for yourself and others; from a victim of circumstance to a powerful creator of your daily reality. So, what is this self acceptance and how to get there? It has been your environment that has dictated how you feel about yourself since Day One. By the time you are an adult, you are armored up to the hilt and on the defensive. When you live in an impenetrable fortress, you inadvertently leave yourself a very small comfort zone to move in. No one else is in it. Definitely not family and friends as they are too close a trigger back to painful old experiences and also most of you yourself are not in it either. Your shadow side is shut out too. This shadow side is the bit you have to explore. Yes there are memories and unpleasant characteristics and feelings but this territory is also home to your greatest potential and gifts. The deep change is that you no longer gauge your life from external reference points - the goal being approval by your peers and survival in your environment. You have moved to an internal reference.

The question to ask is 'How do I feel about this and that?' rather than 'How might this be judged by others?' Over time you will come to recognize yourself as 'usually pretty fair', or someone who's 'intuition serves me well'. Then you are bringing your thoughts in to harmony with all that is the case anyway. Resistance and self doubt, in all their manifestations, fall away. To continue the process of change you are also observing what makes you tick. It might be that you feel strongly about injustice but you might also notice that you yourself have a bit of a persecution complex. There is no longer anyone to blame, not even yourself. Addictions from love, to alcohol, to work no longer have the mental hold over you because peer pressure is less of an influence. Free of outside pressure, you notice, right away, what you do and do not want to do and trust it. When you ask yourself what feels good and understand your cravings as they arise, you can let them go.

Presence as freeing your mind

Do not be fooled in to believing that you have got a great head on your shoulders and that, of everything, your reasoning has never let you down. Look at your thoughts a little more objectively for a moment. They have effectively been waging a war of attrition on your well being, dismissing out of hand any feeling or intuitive insight. How many fleeting visions of imagination do you thwart as they arise, with a judgement like its impossible, that's unlikely, I doubt it or dream on...without actually meaning the latter! What is really going on in your head is a very long or very short medley of tunes on a loop. Some short circuit back to the same song every few minutes or so, others are hoping they can write a new melody but find it strangely familiar after all. We need some discipline around here to mentally move our thoughts from repetitive bias to conscious choice. We have established that we are each just a schism of energy that identifies with countless experiences and beliefs over time. Somehow you end up on this beach with all your baggage, completely disconnected from the ocean of possibilities you emerged from. Then to cap it all, you say to yourself, well this is who I am. I recommend stepping back into the ocean and this can be done by starting to allow a gap between your thoughts - if you don't mind? Brilliant though they are! Although you will experience a loss of imagined control, in its place you will be allowing the infinite organizing power of nature to influence you. Then things really start to get exciting as the parameters of your old identity soften and inspiration rolls in for expression.

Presence in dreams

Dreams are often a way for someone who has died to come and say hello, that they are alright or need some further acknowledgement. Patterns also show up like betrayal, rejection, being incapacitated or exposed in some way. These are all useful to observe in any healing journey, which is nothing more than an ever increasing self awareness. The happy knock on effect is a comfortability with, and compassion for, all living things and their trials and tribulations. In the meantime, your dreams are an arena where what you are afraid of can show up. This does not really narrow it down as people are, on the whole, very afraid of anything out of the ordinary. They can hardly look or listen even when they are awake in case, God forbid! they happen upon something that contradicts the consensus. Fair enough, most people do not want to see spirits all day of people long gone, let alone those of all the animals, but what else are you missing? All of it, I would answer. Fear of hearing something contrary blocks out guidance, for starters, from all aspects of our being, our innate intelligence. God, perhaps, might like to express something even, seeing as he has at least a good bit of perspective. Do not get me started on his omnipresence, omniscience and eternal nature, all of which we have too if we only allowed divine aspects of our being to have a say, rather than just the mundane. We also miss the restorative experience of the countryside, life lessons, foresight and the endless solutions there are, to the difficulties we face. All these things then, for the moment, can only surface in our dreams. Perhaps with your next year's tax returns also compile your dream journal in to a manifesto. Collectively, they would make for the introduction of a lot of new policies and interesting reading. First you have to start keeping one.

Being present in a relationship

Punctuality. If someone is late to meet us it means, on some level, they think their time is more valuable than ours. Each time it happens, it triggers a selection of bad memories and negative thought patterns including low self esteem or anger. If you are late to your place of work, it is fine. They can sack you or make your life miserable and make you pay in some other way. If it is your partner, the trouble is less visible but evident over time. When you get to the pearly gates you will not wish that you spent more time at the office but you may well regret having not prioritized your relationship.

All time keeping problems come down to resistance. Nearly everybody has a chronic problem with it. They have resistance to getting up, resistance to going to work, resistance to communicating and a resistance to spending time, money or energy visiting or caring for people, let alone investing in themselves. Almost last on the list is the partner who is chosen often as the most tolerant of the least attention. In none of the great spiritual texts does it say we were put on the planet to tolerate one another, see what we can get away with and avoid. Be willing. Develop a new attitude that starts the day with an enthusiasm for what and who lies ahead and make a point of being on time for the best things in your diary. Instead of planning to get out of it at the weekend, start getting into it, as of now.

Joint Decision Making. There are hundreds of decisions to be made as we go along. People laugh and say 'Oh, I know who wears the trousers around here' but actually decision making is a question of knowing when to lead and when to follow. It is destructive to bow to the most stubborn, when two heads are better than one. To allow those two heads to work in synergy, they cannot be immersed in a power struggle. I do not mean fighting but one person needing to be heard, the other needing to be right; one person needing to know, another being the responsible one or the one careful with money. They are all imagined roles. Take a chance on trusting each other or yourself - whichever is most unusual.

The main obstacle to relaxed decision making is everyone taking themselves too seriously. Do you honestly think you can pre empt if the child will thrive in one school rather than another; whether the sun will shine enough if you stay local for your holidays; if the car you pick off the internet will be a miraculous classic or an utter let down? The truth is, you cannot know, you cannot control outcomes and it does not really matter. Zig zag off on another tangent, when you need to, but remain determined to enjoy the process. Even lightening your language will set a new tone. Ask 'Shall we chance this?' 'Do you have any particular worries either way?'

Also give each other room to daydream. This is the space for creativity and new ideas to come in. If you do not, decisions can only be made from a narrow, fear-based perspective, by weighing up only what you met in the past. Break some new ground and take some risks together and laugh, rather than point the finger, if they go awry.

Time Together. Many people have not even thought about keeping an attitude of gentleness in their relationships. However, it is only with this spirit of cooperation that harmony is possible. More widespread are expectations, roles and other ideas from the past showing up, to brow beat each other with. The only way to avoid getting lost in internal and external pressures, is to keep seeing the light and good in your companion. This is easier if you do not drink too much when you are together. Drink is a depressant and people often feel victimized and disappointed after it. It is important to release old toxic thoughts because then you have a chance of freedom and experiencing positive patterns of connection in love. To start this, think of your home as a sanctuary where you do not allow any conflict in.

Time together with others. The main risks that send couples into an insular life and the mutual agreement to have no other real friends, are disloyalty and fear of change. I do not necessarily mean disloyalty to the extent of running off to join the circus with someone new and more appealing. Love is setting your happiness in the happiness of another and when you are out socially, this loyalty can be expressed by remaining emotionally aware of your spouse. Fear of change, on the other hand, is one's own affair. If insecurity, jealousy or guilt occur, these are your own triggers from your own psyche that need to be released, cleared, healed. Do whatever you want to do with them but remember they are yours, never caused by the other person. To practice having fun together with others, stay grounded and remember you are only really responsible for yourself.

Bedroom communication. So how is your body language? Is there a back to back companionable 'Na night then' or an edging closer if you want a hug or something more lively? Maybe this winter its about stepping up the chemistry within your own body and enjoying the new synergy that unfolds between you. The question, all too often, is whether you feel attractive enough or still find your partner so. The answer is inevitably, eventually, no. By mistake, you are simultaneously saying no to nearly all the good there is, to inhabiting a physical body. Bonding, comfort and playfulness all out the window, while you are trying to get a bit fitter, find the time or find the feeling. There is an opportunity here far more interesting here than a night study class has to offer. Explore, instead, the health benefits of touch and the foods that are also aphrodisiacs.

Money. A deep feeling of scarcity has come over everyone in the last few years. That does not mean money should become our one priority. Life is still for living, however poor. We are here to make our dreams manifest. Only in this fleeting lifetime can we make what is possible actual, really make things happen. We ourselves are the results of our parents' dreams. So, top priority is to find out each other's dreams. Try to support them and not judge anything as a waste of money! We are on the planet at this time for good reason. Everyone has a contribution to make, be it physical like a coach or emotional like a parent or a mentor. Try not to argue over finances. Conflict will hold you apart and broke! When you get to meet Saint Peter, he won't want to know what you saved...all he'll want to know is what you gave!

Television. Many couples find they have watched twice as much television and done twice as much shopping since they lived together. This is because they are ways to be in each other's company, in time off. Unfortunately, they are both accepted ways to zone out mentally and emotionally too. The shopping is a necessity that sees hundreds of couples head for shopping centres, far and near, when in fact their souls are crying out for some peace, privacy and to be in nature. Even the gym is an environment with strip lighting, machinery and televisions as well, providing more energetic hardship. The divisiveness of watching the television is two fold. First it is not interactive, it is amusement-based and so inspires no engagement from those watching. Secondly, it syphons in vast amounts of images, news and judgements that make people feel bad about themselves and the world. How about, no television two evenings a week and instead dream up a joint creative project to work on, play a game or play some music? The songs your partner picks out as a compilation and sound track will tell you a much, much more interesting story than any soap or crime scene investigation.

Food. When we cook, our intention is to replenish our miraculous, graceful bodies...or may be its not. Sometimes, we are looking for something quick and easy to eat. Sometimes we are led by our cravings or trying to come up with something all the family will like. Try and include amino acids, omegas, enzymes, anti aging ingredients, brain food, fibre, minerals, vitamins and a full spectrum pro biotic and seaweed'. If you aim high like this, you will be well. In Ockanawa, they have an average life span of 100 years. Sweet potatoes are central to their diet. Whether its simple foods or a complex mix, conceived by herbalists centuries ago, we have all the secrets to eternal youth. So lets stop rolling along from breakfast roll to 'meat and two veg' dinners. The next level of consciousness is holding the awareness that if it is meat now, it was an animal before. That means that many people, stuck in the old paradigm, are picking up spiritual grievances at every meal.

As your empathy expands to all living things, you will find you want to be as harmless as possible, in your life choices. Many people, who work with animals, see their consciousness as superior to humans. This is in many ways including love, loyalty, gentleness, family bonds, senses and emotional intelligence. In the past, these faculties have been rated lower than cognitive powers. That is only in the recent past, though. Further back, the aborigines and other tribes identified and lived by 36 senses, valuing and utilizing them all. If you end up eating nothing animal-related, your spirit starts to soar and health problems disappear, which might be worth an experimental period in the kitchen.

Sex. Making love is of course no one's business but your own. Nonetheless, I will add my ideas. Consider, what are the top ten things that switch you on? It would be a pity not to know them as everyone has at least ten. The biggest challenge for most people is to move their focus from what turns them off. Work can be a passion killer as is the world news. A wakeful child or a disorientated parent can preoccupy most lobes in the brain too. If you are clear on your ten things though, you will develop a habitual responsiveness, receptivity and appreciation when one of them crosses your radar. Stay alert. Do not miss the moment. Also a healthy sense of self helps. This is usually accompanied by the philosophy 'If its not fun I'm not doing it'.

Being Present To An Environment

First, decide to acknowledge every aspect of the scene as you go along. When driving, dead animals might be the first thing you notice. If you see a rabbit on the road, at the Bright Eyes stage of its life, acknowledge, for a moment, all animals killed on the road. In a sense, send them some love. This goes a long way to releasing their trauma and maybe their soul. It is important not to be traumatized though, yourself, by everything you witness or you will just create more of it. Draw the line, as well, at clearing bugs on the windscreen and sending them to the light, or you will never get a break.

As you approach your home or town, clear your own relationship to the place. Notice your feelings and initial thoughts like 'Its a pain having to come here' or 'Everyone's so miserable here'. Let the thoughts go and start to look for positive aspects. Then you are engaging your energy productively, to bring clarity, peace or light in some shape or form. This way one can transform somewhere like Carlow Town into a desirable destination like Monte Carlo.

Clear the karma for where you spend your time too. One of the ways to stay grounded, while tuning in to dense environmental and metaphysical energies, is to listen to music. Songs like In My Life by The Beatles are particularly good. They can say what you mean to say but can often not quite think of how to. Music also keeps your mood high and bright and less susceptible to sinking into vortices!

Pay attention to what your senses are telling you. Are you freezing when its not that cold? Are you claustrophobic when you are apparently on your own with plenty of space? These are all indicators of atmospheres around you. Do not let them close in and mistake them for your own condition. Clear them.

Learn to pivot your experience from one of darkness and foreboding to one of light and vision. As much as a place can be heavy with the past, each place is simultaneously a medium within which you can follow your dreams. You can create your own little piece of heaven. Everywhere can be mellow and inspiring. You do not have to leave, you can simply harmonize your current environment.

When you focus on a place you will spot some of its associations with the past. This might be as concrete as finding old pottery in the mud or it could be less tangible like the hairs on your neck standing on end. But also remember how transient we are. When you stay in a yurt or tent, or the tide washes away your footprints on the beach, it is as simple as that too.

Think of tin mines, gold mines and coal mines. Notice quarries and road building. The earth is effectively left wide open and there has been a lot of disturbance to it. Every country has areas like this and the earth is deserving of your attention to it. As with all matters great and small, your attention is enough. You will get better and better at letting things go. However, to start with, you will feel inordinately tired after very little space clearing.

There is much geopathic stress everywhere. It is a current of energy much denser than the human fields. It is often caused by environmental features like an underground stream crossing a fault line of gamma radiation. Unbeknown to the residents of a house, their bodies may well be struggling to cope with this grave interruption to their own life force. At best, our frequency is around 5 hertz. Geopathic stress has been recorded up to 1000 hertz. Findings of diviners in the past have identified links with cot death, learning difficulties, cancers and heart disease and been able to accurately detect which part of the body an illness will have occurred. The conscious process is exactly the same to clear this energy, ask for it to disperse harmlessly back into oneness.

With places so densely populated and for so long, there is also a high rate of spiritual disturbances. One priest commented that if he was to respond to every chronic problem of this nature, he would be on the road twenty four hours a day, seven days a week, blessing houses and conducting exorcisms. This, again, is not as specialized a procedure as people think. The only risk is going in to fear. If you can stay in your powerful understanding of how energy works, everything can be healed equally easily and successfully. Every spiritual turbulence, however violent, is rooted in unacknowledged grief. It may have been generations back. In a stronger and stronger attempt to be noticed, energies get denser and more volatile. Your job remains the same though, to systematically acknowledge and release the pain through compassion.

To recognize who and what needs acknowledgement, you must not go into reaction. Reaction is the opposite of response. It is personal, fearful and unconscious instead of objective, compassionate and conscious. It becomes a great adventure meeting spirits and places like this. You will come away on a high, delighted with having facilitated healing for problems that had been entrenched and fractious for years. Relationships heal, family feuds resolve, depressions lift, bankruptcy is avoided and long term pain finally shifts. At times you will need to pull over on your way home and sleep for a while. That is because you are processing a lot of difficult information, albeit briefly.

Sometimes you can help hundreds of people that never really left, move on. Get skillful at identifying and witnessing specific eras and illness. Maybe they died of smallpox or in battle. Send them to the light. Experiment with numbers. Perhaps a mission to clear the 60,000 lost souls from the Battle of the Boyne, although I think that clearing is complete.

Explore ancient places to expand your consciousness. As you approach a place, feel the pulse emanating from it. Even if it is only an old well or a path. There is a continual reflection between you and your environment. If you are not resonating well, the power of ancient places can trigger fear, chaos and violence. This means, avoid setting up a sanctuary, visitor centre, let alone a home, in the vicinity of such a place.

Notice as well, what you attract, by way of experience. You might be hoping to find pockets of happiness, where you would learn a thing or two about love and acceptance but then, what you meet might be something quite different. You will be amazed how many people no longer even go upstairs in their own home, sleep in separate bedrooms from their partner and who see themselves as completely the innocent bystander in the whole thing - a victim of circumstance! Space clearing is therefore a useful way to introduce new ideas to people who are too upset to take responsibility for anything at first. If you can make a difference to someone's home, they start to feel slightly empowered and confident that things could change in other areas of their life. They get interested in the energetic world and how to participate in it, successfully. From there, they can start to accept responsibility for their own creations and enjoy the subsequent power of embarking on future ones. The order of events you can apply is witness, clear, stay present, help and accept.

You will see the spectrum of experience people live with. Some live in great hardship and some millionaires. Some millionaires in fact who fear great hardship and some hard up people with large-scale dreams, fit for a king. There are some with great influence and some with great commitment. Everyone has skills and qualities. What you will notice, though, is that every last person you meet is really fraught. Your fresh perspective will be literally brand new to most. You are energetically letting people breathe again, move on, make changes and commune with their environment.

Try to emphasize that there is literally nothing outside ourselves to blame. No danger outside ourselves to fear. There is also nothing to hate or even judge as bad. It is all just residual bad feeling. It is coming to the surface, nothing more. Even these bad feelings are a blessing. They are not supposed to be overwhelming and lead to crisis. We are supposed to recognize these moments as wonderful opportunities for healing.

It does not naturally occur to people to spot fear as it arises in oneself. They rush straight to focussing on what the perceived danger is. It becomes attached to a story line in one's own life, like fear of having an accident, not having enough money or getting ill and then its chewed over, like a pit bull terrier with a rag doll. Try not to take everything personally. No one sees their ideas for what they are. Thoughts, fears, horrors, cruelty and differences are just persistent waves breaking on a shore. We just have to let them pull out again, as they naturally do. People have to stop fighting it or running up the beach to higher ground. It is actually harder to stop fighting for righteous causes than fighting to let off steam. The good causes and the great reasons and the deep feelings evoked are all relevant but our job, as human beings, is not to fight and hold up the resolution process. Instead, total surrender is called for and complete forgiveness.

As you spend time listening to yourself amongst new people, you will be shown many things about your own shadowy parameters too. Frustrations, indecision and defensiveness will no doubt show up. Come to accept these energies as part of a perfect combination, that is you. You will eventually stop giving one more credibility, as your identity, than others.

One might have thought that people would be in a hurry to learn how to support themselves emotionally and mentally, but sadly not. For most, personal pain is embedded in so many layers of, apparently valid, tragic information and logic that it has become the very fabric of their being. It has become essentially a true story or a self fulfilling prophecy. This hidden pain has been mirrored back so consistently in one's experience that they fully believe the pain is not their own but actually an objective reality. When you are present, you are holding a space open for clarity and healing. It is the real beauty of an energetic universe, it is completely fluid, silken and oceanic. Nothing is really stuck or damaged, so do not fall for the illusion that it is, however convincing or nerve-wracking.

Three specific clearings that apply in most contexts are returning a place from chaos to clarity, from conflict to peace and from lack to abundance. When consciously being present to an environment, it helps to have a vision of harmonious existence, in your mind. All clarity is more purposeful than any amount of wishing away the disharmony you see.

It is a balancing act, setting out to clear the energy of a home. You have to hope a moment arises when a person can reconnect with their sense of humour, lighten up and experience self awareness, without despondency. You will always go into some deep subjects about the inhabitants, flora and fauna and animals. Everything will bring up a serious social commentary, such as history of abuse or environmental deterioration or something. This can be even more tiring than dense land energies, because people want to pour over the details, one more time. Do not let them. Alight, acknowledge and move on.

Staying present can also take its toll on one's nervous system. This is because you spend so much time around chaotic situations, reminding people of an underlying moment of calm. It is prudent, therefore, to clear yourself afterwards, of 1) Any information that you met unconsciously. 2) Any adverse effects. 3) Your etheric energy field. Problems only take up residence in the etheric field. It is not your problem until you make it yours. Unravel the energetic, spiritual complex that has brought you to identify with anything. Do not carry it a moment longer.

Chapter Six
Oneness

Remembering oneness via music

If your life was a piece of music, how would it sound? What rhythm do you keep? Have you managed to change tempo or, even harder, keep time in a duet? Many life events make you syncopated, erratic and inconsistent. People stop and start, one step forward, two steps back; kind, defensive; brave, feeble. With awareness, you can align any skipped beat, just by replacing doubt with unwavering faith. This is the amazing thing about knowing that the world and all its goings on is one energetic fluid mass. It is the grand piano of experience; all the instruments of the orchestra in one. This means that all we have to do is listen to the frequency and tone we are making. Given attention, we can hear very well the notes come into harmony. Notice discord, ask for harmony and love the melody.

Remembering oneness via swimming

This is a detoxification through relaxing your energetic boundaries. The water muffles any sound and there is room to lie completely still. When you have been somewhere busy, like work or a supermarket, you can come to the shore or a pool to restore your equilibrium. Any emotional information, you have met, washes away. Any environmental toxicity loses its grip. This time, it is not about distance or speed. It is about immersion and stillness. Often people try and push each other to exercise or compete. They do not realize that effortless ease is the real measure of success, the true sign of health, flexibility and fitness. Like a leaf on a river, we can float downstream, carried relatively carefully by mother nature and with all our companions colourfully twinkling around us, in an autumnal way. Yes, it means you do not have much control but you do have infinite, back to back, opportunities to relax. Practice this immersion and it will become an acceptance. Practice this acceptance and it will become a joy. Practice this joy and you will create a better reality, in and out of the water.

Remembering oneness via meditation

Love is not an emotion or a benevolence. Love is a state of being that encompasses everyone and everything at the same time. Gentleness is a tangible semblance of what love might be and so you can learn how to get your body into that state. At the beginning of guided meditations, someone always says something like 'Relax the body, release any tension from the legs, the arms, breathe quietly and deeply'. This is softening the body and develops an interactive bridge between mind, body and spirit. The body becomes aware of a field of energy, larger than your physical parameters. You miraculously realize you are not only physical, you are also light. Think this and feel this often in the day. When you bring gentleness to mind and body, they stop opposing each other, for a time. Meditation can be worked on methodically and mechanically but it is already doing you good, right from the start.

Sit, stand or lie comfortably. You do not need to slow the body down or make the mind quiet. That would lead to an escape of sorts, in the form of falling asleep probably. Or would lead to a dumbing down of the negative emotions. The key is to stay mindful of what arises. By noticing good and bad with equanimity, the mind moves into line with the impulses of the heart. Do not sigh or hurry or strain. Learning to govern your breath is extremely powerful. Because your lungs and breathing represent your life force, by making them conscious, you are literally directing your energy and thoughts in the direction you want your life to go. No more reeling from pillar to post, aiming for one thing, inadvertently creating another.

You can even choose your air, when you breathe in. Take in only the best. Transmute the air that seems to be available to you. If you are sitting in traffic, do not breathe in the fumes. Breathe in Swiss mountain air; breathe in warm clear air from the Anza Borego desert; breathe in the scent from the winter jasmine, in the garden. Yes, it is a choice and you have the whole world to play with, as it is all one and the same energy field. Your outward breath expresses who you are, so make it the best of who you are. Living and breathing positively, makes you a breath of fresh air for your surroundings too.

Remembering oneness via love
Explore the roles of lover, beloved and love itself. As the contractions in your heart ease and the conscious space within you grows, you will receive and be able to hold more and more loving information. That means, you do not have to stay as you always were. Instead of saying, 'I'm not a romantic person', or 'I do not understand mysticism or poetry', you become more open-minded. You will resonate at a new level that easily incorporates whatever frequencies you meet. At first it will be ideas, signs and creative impulses. They can be processed and accepted almost intellectually, simply by clearing your mental

energy. The deeper love information, when it starts to pour in, may meet more resistance in you. This is because it triggers something more painful.

In the past, you could blame your childhood or circumstances. As you come to understand that you have created all of it, you blame yourself. This polarizing from one negative emotion to another, blame to regret, is not the answer. Go beneath the drama and opposites of right and wrong and yours or mine and keep remembering the more fundamental unity. Just because you are not familiar with unbridled passion or oceanic bliss, complete trust or endless curiosity, does not mean they are not there. You hold the full spectrum of energy within each of your cells. It is only fear that keeps you remote. The key is to notice and accept all of it, as it shows up, in you or anyone else. Start to recognize the vast potential contained within each person.

If you can live open-heartedly, you can be involved in an epic collaboration. This could be on a scale capable of reversing pollution, ending war and sustaining economic enterprise. If you stay in the illusion of being separate, nothing can change. This is because you will have failed to understand the universe and can only hope to cope with what happens. What happens will only be more of the same, because you will not have shifted your creative energy from unconscious to conscious. With love in your heart, you can live every moment on purpose.

How distance healing works
As you start to feel the wave of vitality and relief from clearing your energy, you will immediately think of ten other people who could really do with it. It might be a parent or child that is down or an infuriating boss or a miserable

work environment with no natural daylight. Everything and everyone is crying out for some love and recognition and you now know how to do it. Do not let doubts creep in. Even if the person is miles away, you can interact with them. Even if they would be highly resistant to anything other than a scientific approach, you can help them. If the place is in another country, you can still find and dissipate toxicity and balance the energy. Even if the events happened decades or even centuries ago, healing can be complete and lasting.

Remember that everyone can heal. In compassionate mode, we are everywhere all at once, healing turbulence in the energetic whole whether its being experienced by one man or a whole planet. All that, just by being peacefully present. There is a challenge implicit in this though: Can you make yourself accept the dark things too; abuse, wars, pollution, cruelty, injustice and starvation? It is not a case of tolerance gone mad, as you might think. You actually perpetuate, strengthen, invite and even necessitate an offensive outcome, if you feel strongly against it. The old truism, what you resist persists. Let the pendulum swing until it rests, on each situation that gets you psyched up. Do not add any particular story to it this time or you will block the healing, by intensifying the emotional charge around the topic. Just hold the understanding that you are letting it go for the greater good. Energetically, if you clear your heart of bad feeling, you are going a long way to lessening it for everyone else.

Chapter Seven

Conscious Creation

In the clearing process, we have moved from head to heart, judgment to healing. Now we come to positive change and manifesting, our energy must move from an attraction to drama to a conscious vision. Everyone has heard of the law of attraction with a brief understanding of it, such as 'Like attracts like' or 'You create what you think about'. Furthermore, many people sense that they must try and think positively or they will draw more negativity in. However, there is a distinct lack of mastery of this law. It is the exception rather than the rule when someone relates the story, "I focused on getting a 6 figure-salaried job and visualized myself still having the time to enjoy the renumeration and within a year that was exactly what was happening." In fact I've never heard that, but definitely some more 'realistic' success stories.

If I mention the law of gravity, there seems to be more consistency in our evidence. Everything always falls if you drop it, whether its heavy or light. Defying the law of gravity, though, are airplanes. They can fly because some people understand the sub laws that have a bearing on the law of gravity; such as lift, thrust and momentum. I hope you will familiarize yourself with and practice the following sub laws to the law of attraction. It will culminate in the same consistency as you can rely on airlines for. 99.999% of flights make it! to their destination. What you will be making is the life you want.

The first sub law is the law of ignorance. The application of this is to notice that you do not KNOW of any solution to your problems but then spend another few moments accepting that you also do not KNOW that there isn't one. Allowing the possibility is not unrealistic, it is literally an acknowledgement of what you cannot know. This regular practice lets in hope, via the side door, as it gives your thoughts a few minutes off from fully convinced gloom and doom. There are sixteen sub laws, so try and get this one up and running right away. If you are so lost in the inevitability of how deep your problems run or a belief that they are all caused by someone else not you, go back to the beginning and clear that.

Having accepted a level of ignorance as to what is actually possible, the second sub law to mastering the law of attraction is that of realization. Nearly everyone has realized that things are changing. Some say there are not as many customers or they will not be going on holiday. They would be glad of a night off at this stage, let alone a night away. Simultaneously, thank God, people have realized that money is not the be all and the end all. There are lots of family outings happening, people helping each other out and home improvements going on. The realization that you must work on, though, is grander than all these. It is; For every desire that exists in the world, there also exists a full realization of that desire. Really let it dawn on you. There is an unlimited number of things and experiences arriving all the time. Everything is possible. So whatever the challenge you are facing, keep in mind that a totally satisfactory outcome exists. It does not matter if its financial, health related, relational or a problem facing the whole world. Let the realization that there is definitely a solution cheer you up every day.

The third addition to mastering the law of attraction, is the sub law of anticipation. Once you have realized that the world holds many possibilities that would solve everything, you must start to get a spring in your step. This will feel like a new optimistic air, replacing the habitual anticipation of impending disaster, or things going from bad to worse, at least. This is important because you are raising your expectations from that of Eeyore, in

Winny The Pooh, expecting rain from his own personal rain cloud...to that of, say, Buzz Light Year of Toy Story, always on his way 'To infinity and beyond'. Remember that what you think about, comes about, so make sure you are anticipating breakthroughs and miraculous triumph over adversity. If you do not deliberately raise your energy like this, you will only be attracting more unhealthy situations to deal with. As you wait, with great excitement and curiosity, say to yourself 'All good things are coming my way'.

Now you know there is an answer and feel the surge of energy to go looking for it, we come to the fourth sub law to mastering the law of attraction; seeking. It is obvious at the moment that however much you need money, the way to get it is not to go out and look for a job. Nor is it to notice a clever little niche in the market and design a labour saving device. Nor is it to start a band and try and reach massive popularity. The answer should be sought inside yourself. Take some quiet moments to reflect on what you actually want, what you are naturally good at and what you really care about. Reaching clarity about these three creates a powerful concoction of intention and ability. It is the only reliable way to establish a productive way forwards. Many people find they cannot listen to themselves and only hear the ideas indoctrinated by their parents, church or the media. This is understandable but it is still no way to live. So, if you would like your own mind back and to expel the effects of the past or a troubled childhood, keep clearing as you go along.

The fifth sub law is that of decision. Now would be a good moment to make the crucial decision to only focus on solutions. It does not matter if you do not know yet exactly what they are. Keep remembering this decision and do not let yourself drift back into focusing on the problem. A problem has a completely different vibration to its solution. They do not even cohabit the same part of the mind. However closely you look at a difficulty, you will never find the inspiration within it to change it. You will simply expand the problem, by giving it more attention and more of your energy. Worse again, you are putting yourself in the wrong mental state for trouble shooting. You render yourself depressed and powerless, which can only invite more of the same subdued outcomes. When you decide not to put yourself down anymore and commit yourself to keeping your eyes peeled for opportunities, then they will arrive thick and fast. A practice to develop might be lateral thinking, such as jotting down twenty money making ideas. The first six will be the ones you always come up with, squeezing the next fourteen out will generate much amusement and no doubt some surprising nuggets of possibility.

The next thing to notice and act on are the discoveries you make. Discovery is the sixth sub law. You are learning how to make your life work for you. Most people observe other people's lives more than their own. However, it is within your experience and your knowledge that you will find the only way forward that is true to you; joyful, fulfilling, interesting and successful for you. It is different for everyone. What anybody else has or does not have is nothing to do with us. Any comparisons will take you off your centre but, until you get out of the habit of comparing yourself to others, practice praising success wherever you see it. Then at least you are keeping your attention on the positive. So, back to you. The sorts of things you will discover are old forgotten talents, people skills, hobbies and studies. You will know which discovery is the key to unlock the challenge you face because of immediate coincidences that follow. You may be offered a free studio space to work in, asked to help a child via grinds, see an advert for something. I guarantee, if you start to appreciate who you are and what makes you tick, you will discover why you are the best candidate for the job of creating your reality.

We are gradually moving ourselves in the mental framework for achieving consistent success. The seventh sub law to mastering the law of attraction is clearing. This is obviously a bit of a speciality for us at this stage. Once you have discovered what you are good at and what you want to do, you must set about clearing any old ideas you believe that would stop you taking the action to bring the positive changes about. These ideas would usually include fear of failure, success, unworthiness, change and loss of identity. In fact fear of nearly everything. To make real change you will also probably need to clear your family history, if it includes abuse or poverty and cultural discriminations between men, women, young, old, race or education. For mastery, I would go as far as to say, though, that you need to clear your whole mind because it has become a seriously muddy pool of clouded judgements. It does not matter how much clear thinking and positive energy you pour in, it will be green and polluted instantly. As this is the pool of thoughts you draw on every morning for refreshment, put time aside to do a complete dredge and install a filter system to ensure you allow only the best for yourself, from now on.

The next sub law is visualization and you might find that you are the first to foresee the worst case scenario. Many people are even paid to quickly appraise a situation and make a projection of the worst outcomes possible. For example, health and safety professionals, first aiders and even managers in every field are expected to only make cautious estimates. When you understand this universal law of attraction, you realize that what you forecast is exactly what you get. Unfortunately, nearly everyone is forecasting drama and disaster. Repeatedly, people push away sustainability by focusing on the recession. On a personal level, many push away their relationship by imagining an eventual repeat of past hurts. Once you have a clear mind, you can start to pull out different images to give your attention to.

All you need to get started is a handful of magazines, maybe not newspapers as they contain an information overload, and cut out every image that appeals in some way. It might be a holiday destination, a smile, a recipe, a boat, a car, a figure, a building, a surfing scene, a party, a phone, a sofa and anything else. Then put them in a box and glance at them from time to time. What you are doing is out-picturing what you see in your life currently and planting seeds of what you would like to see. What you see, touch, smell and everything else now is just what your thoughts created in the past. Expand your ideas for your future and just watch how it all comes along.

Release is the ninth sub law. Surrender the task of manifesting to nature or the bigger picture or God. Notice for a moment how your thoughts plough on. Perhaps you are worried about someone in your family or feeling bad about something that was said to you. Do not pollute your own mind with any negativity. See it for what it is, a challenging experience, and let it go. The release technique I like is to ask 'Do you know what to do about that? No. Are you beating yourself up about it? Yes. Would you beat up someone else if they did not know what to do? No. Are you willing to let some of that self disapproval go? Yes. And a bit more? Yes. And are you ready to give yourself some approval? Yes. And a bit more? Yes. And a bit more? Yes.' Funny as it may sound, this is an extremely effective way to bypass your habitual brain patterns and appreciate yourself again. Slapping yourself about, internally, just doesn't get the results.

Releasing, in its context as a sub law to mastering the law of attraction, is slightly different. Once you have decided what you want and start taking steps towards success, you have to release your attachment to reaching your goal or receiving your large stash of cash or whatever you asked for. Trust that it is coming your way. I can hear people groan at the word 'trust'. They think that nothing happens if they do not make it happen, or nothing happens because someone else will not let it happen. Neither is the case. A release technique for this is to say 'I have sent out a request for the best possible outcome and I will now just gladly accept what comes.' Keep yourself light and receptive because that is all a human being truly is anyway.

The tenth sub law to use is that of one mind. This is our new paradigm thinking, accepting that we are all one. To get our individual heads around this, accept first that the smallest unit of all things is energy. That goes for everything on earth and in space. The human body is one creation out of that pool of energy but literally everything emerges out of it. This great fluid catalogue of possibilities has, for a long time, been a source of healing. As you work with energy you find you can just ask for a realignment of an imbalanced creation, like an injury, and correct it there and then. This is because we are interacting with this fluid field, not the solid, apparently damaged, flesh and bone body.

In terms of the law of attraction, plus our intention to consistently achieve what we set out for, the one mind is even more superb. There is nowhere where there is no energy. Even though you might feel low in energy, you actually contain enough energy to light a whole city for a week, you just have to become aware of your participation in this one mind. Furthermore, all energy is equally magnificent as it holds within it every possibility. Where we humans have the advantage is that we have this awareness and can literally draw forth what we want from this cosmic soup. Nothing is impossible or even difficult. Just look for the need and ask for the inspiration to meet it. It already exists and was just waiting for you to ask. Download whatever you want for yourself and others.

Sub law, number eleven, is objective. Become a person with great focus who instinctively keeps their eyes on their objective. There are three ingredients. First, worry not as to how exactly you will manifest something. The one universal intelligence has countless ways of bringing things about much more readily than you could come up with. A useful phrase to keep your objective clear and the means to get there unlimited is to say thank you. 'Thank you for taking care of all my bills', 'Thank you for my healing', Thank you for ... Fill in the space with whatever vast altruistic wish or personal dream, you have come up with.

Secondly, keeping your thoughts on your objective, means not letting them go back to past successes or failures. This is it, right now; you are a grown up, in your most powerful position so far to carve out the life you want. Do not victimize yourself by saying you cannot, never could, never will be able to or they won't let me.

The third aspect of objective is as an opposite to subjective. When you are subjective, you are saying I need this and that, I am this and that, I want this and that...but, in reality, you are not that small. When you are objective, you are saying 'As a participator in this massive intelligent energy field, I choose this and I choose that'. This is the key to conscious creations that will reliably benefit you and everyone else.

Private and confidential. The sub law of secrecy. Some people are very keen to share an idea as soon as it comes to them. They feel like they are sharing the enthusiasm and optimism of having found a solution, even if it is still at the concept stage. In fact, you should keep your goals to yourself at first. This serves to preserve the seed of change. However, do let your own excitement and strategy develop. Make some investigations and paint a picture in your imagination of how you would like things to turn out. That might be a job application or a look at courses or a book under your pillow. Pay close attention to the seedlings you are growing but keep them close to your chest until they show forth fruit.

Thirteenth is the law of reserve. Think of yourself, for a moment, as a huge reservoir, maybe stretching a mile across. Your edges are concrete and your water is dark blue and silver with occasional white horses and many ducks gathering on the far side. On the nearside, there are fifty little dinghies and a hundred youngsters come every afternoon, in their life jackets, to sail around buoys, race and practice retrieving 'man overboard!' Life is good; sailing skills improve, friendships blossom and ducklings arrive. You offer your water to everyone and yet nothing depletes your supply. Pipes draw gallons to households in the city nearby and the rain replenishes your levels to the brim again. You are a nature reserve. You can only be successful if you value yourself as such. Maintain your boundaries and welcome only healthy living pursuits.

The fourteenth sub law is nourishment, so at last we come to sustainability. When we describe someone as malnourished, we suppose they are both impoverished and neglected. Hardship and ignorance are the same two atmospheres we put around our dreams though too. We assume they will be hard to achieve and we do not know how to pursue them. On this sort of fallow soil, nothing much can grow. The sort of nourishment needed is encouragement. This is from the inside out, from you, not waiting for external support. Mentally, this will mean feeding your mind with positive imagery. Physically, it will mean investing time and action, every day. Emotionally, it will mean loving what you are doing and making yourself laugh. Your spiritual nourishment takes the form of gratitude. This attitude literally facilitates your interaction with the great sea of possibilities there are. You are letting the universe know what you want and how glad you are of it. These, in combination, are a feast for your creative force.

We are at the penultimate law to mastery. You have set out your desires with great clarity, cleared all the self defeating habits and beliefs from your past and are racing towards your goal. It feels good, you smile at your partner every morning and say 'I am so grateful everything always works out for us'. You are very very close to mastering the law of attraction. You are remembering that the better the story you tell of your life, the better your life gets. Be ready, though, to acknowledge resistance when it arises. A law of resistance might sound, at first, more like Sod's Law or Murphy's Law. Until now, when you met a pitfall, a hold up or an obstacle you will, no doubt, have had one of two reactions. Either, feeling thwarted and asking yourself 'What is the point? It was never going to happen anyway, or bloody-minded perseverance; 'Do I look bothered? I'm carrying on, if it kills me'. There is a third way though. The understanding we actually need to have of resistance is that it is crucial, positive and a very good indicator that change is really happening. Any negativity around resistance will only block progress. If you welcome resistance in any form, you will start to get the consistent results

72

you have been priming yourself for. What you touch will turn to gold as long as you do not stop the transformation every time it gets uncomfortable.

The sixteenth sub law is mastery itself. It is almost the most important sub law to making the law of attraction work for you. This is because you must agree to being the powerful conductor of your own orchestra, rather than continue playing second fiddle in a cacophony of white noise. If you think you are hopeless and stuck, you are. When you know yourself to be an evolving masterpiece, you are. You are being offered the most valuable power of all, to direct your thoughts. These sub laws are a training in mindful participation and conscious creativity. You will steadily progress in your awareness of initial ignorance; through to noticing revelations; through hopeful anticipation; seeking solutions; decision making; discovery; energy clearing; out-picturing current situations; release; participating in the one whole energy field; keeping a focus on your objective; secrecy until you see it happen; valuing yourself as a nature reserve; nourishment for all aspects of your being; resistance as a good thing; through to this - mastery. Every experience is of your design, so you are now at the end of a cycle of victimization in your life. It is a time of transition, savour every moment and trust that you are now in a flow of good chi.

Chapter Eight

Intuition

It is intuition that is guiding your energy fields to release toxicity, guiding your heart to make good choices and guiding your mind as to what to create next. As you become confident at returning to stillness, develop your intuitive faculty. After many decades of listening to your head; practical considerations, external pressures and notions limited by fear, it is important to deepen your sense of self. You are much more than these mental and emotional processes. One way to do this is to identify which spiritual beings you believe in or are at least interested in.

If you grew up Christian, work with the trio; God, Mary and Jesus or God, Jesus and the Holy Spirit. You can include saints, Joseph, the donkey that carried Mary and any other guides from the Bible stories, that resonate with you. Saint Germain can instantly balance male and female energy. Saint Paul helps with mystical surrender to the divine. It is not to start believing in another system and more characters from the past but to start listening to the spiritual aspects of yourself. They are there and they are as real and reliable as any of your critical apparatus. They are much more so, in fact, as rather than a deconstructionist energy, they offer an overview of the bigger picture, the greater good and a unified means of navigation through your life.

As you start to listen to your intuitive team, in their many forms, every polarized occurrence and difficult decision is replaced with a personal choice you can trust. Once you fully understand that divine aspects of life are working through you as much as, if not more than, old favourites like Freudian oppression, depression, suppression et al, your experience will grow to incorporate this expansion. No longer give any airtime to ideas like 'Have I messed up here?' or 'Should I try harder?' They are old paradigm, disconnected perspectives. You are more resourceful than that, you are consciously participating in life's whole rich tapestry.

Activate as many previously unrealized aspects of the self you can: Your inner team might include Nike. She flies a little like superman except with an arm up - hence the tick shape of the Nike symbol. She was a goddess of something in the past, victory maybe or games. Then there are the Pleiades, that group of stars, also known as the Seven Sisters. The stars emanate a 5th dimensional understanding. They illuminate events in the light of acceptance and unconditional love. I understand them as being continuously in clearing mode. With access to these, you can return to stillness within seconds of an interruption or worrisome thought. In your group of divine aspects, you could also have angels. Incorporate Fhelyai, angel of animals and upload that immense power, wild and domestic. Also Archangel Michael, Sandalphon and Metatron - the latter two are twins and are each the size of the earth. Then there is Azrael, angel of grief; Daniel the angel of marriage; Sarah, a healing angel; Uriel and Ariel, angels of nature and thousands more. You will find that each one seems to be able to instantly intervene on any matter. Every religion of the world holds gems of insight that you can access. For example, the understanding that only Allah is perfect. The central Rastafarian beliefs, harmlessness, celebration and gratitude. The Hindu understanding of karma can remind us not to personalize others' suffering. This better allows healing from a neutral standpoint.

One of the occupational hazards of invoking and activating countless powerful aspects of oneself is that your own worst nightmares show up. It might be poltergeist activity, a flood, a swarm of flies or a trapped, unspecified creature in the gutter. You will learn again and again that what inner guidance actually does is create opportunities for growth and healing. You are being shown the invisible ceiling and parameters you have operated within to date, usually fear-related. The job of your intuitive team is not to protect from some external world and create a padded cell for you but instead to expand us beyond what we know so far. Everything can be resolved as you go along by acknowledging and clearing energetically. You can also ask a simple question like 'How many worst nightmares am I still holding?' and clear those.

Sirius is another constellation that can also inform you intuitively. Beings from there emanate a sixth dimensional understanding, of the structure of reality. Interaction with this dimension leads to understanding the tetrahedral arrangement of the heart muscles and their limitless ability to resonate a lamina flow. This is a current that travels in a different direction to mass consciousness, but creates no turbulence or conflict. It reminds us how hugely superior the heart is to the mind, which cannot seem to help itself arguing over the details. The sacred geometry that underlies every form, as a structure of light, also exists in this sixth dimension. Therefore, if given your intuitive attention, previously unmanifest objects and situations can take shape. You are literally drawing something actual from the field of possibilities.

The right mood for being present
What is compassion one might ask? Is it not just something for Mother Teresa or Florence Nightingale? Or is it not just ordinary kindness? That would do nicely except that ordinary kindness is a bit like common sense. It is not that common. Compassion can be understood as a combination of these two things - common sense and ordinary kindness. Get them operative in your daily life. First start to use your senses, to really see, hear, touch and feel. They are common enough faculties but assumptions get in the way of the sensory information really having an impact on us. These assumptions are the consensus, what society or the media say is going on, rather than assessing information for yourself. We are anesthetized from really caring

about it too, so really using your senses and keeping your heart open, with a compassionate perspective, may be brand new.

As well as only believing what the consensus has told us, you may not have been listening at all. Historically, we have tried to impose our will on the world, rather than listen to and allow what life has in store for us. When we live in our senses, at least occasionally, we are inclined towards the appropriate response of ordinary kindness. This is the opposite of resistance, where your energy is geared up to trying to come up with a different outcome. Who are we to think we can come up with a better master plan than nature? The objective then is to get back in touch with it. Stay alert, trusting that what is happening should be happening. Get ready to respond and take part. It cannot be any worse than fighting our experience every day; fighting for justice or recognition or a few extra euro. Live as nature intends, then you are bound to be successful.

A further understanding of nature can be gained by uploading goddess energy into your intuitive team of guides. Along with the others Kwan Yin, for example, can help. It is unlikely that she, or any other divine feminine energy, will have been an accepted part of your judgement before now. In the consensus that people have lived with, most mainly feminine traits like intuition, nurturance, patience and forgiveness have been equated with weakness. In the media, women are mainly portrayed as victims of violence and abuse. This demeans the very sort of intelligence that is needed by both men and women. We have established that forgiveness and intuition are, in fact, the only navigational tools available to get back to a sense of interconnectedness. Plus they provide the will and means to care for each other and our environment in a meaningful way. As we are all one, these are only superficially feminine aspects; masculine traits such as leadership, authority, and protectiveness are also available to both genders, of all ages, in any life circumstance.

As you explore, keep remembering two fundamental dynamics. Firstly, everything in life is a reflection of something in you. So, clear whatever it is in yourself that conflicts are reflecting and bathe in the reflected glory of the good times, respectively. Secondly, remember that you are the one holding problems in place. These might be emotions, beliefs or environmental programming. No need to find out exactly which dimension of your being is hanging on and perpetuating situations, just ask to let go. This will help you recognize that everything in life, without exception, is a gift. It brings the gift of greater self awareness. You notice quickly what you have created and because you are present you can let it go. This way, you do not drag everything into your future with you. Instant healing is also at work. One form of consciousness, the mind, is spontaneously amending another form of consciousness, the body. You are literally making peace. A fragmented consciousness manifests conflict and illness. So sometimes a blanket clearing, from fragmentation to wholeness is called for.

Embodiment of presence

If the awareness and clearing has become a way of life, you will already be receptive to the people, conflicts and opportunities that present themselves. The next step is to embody that clarity. The difference will be apparent in your every movement and action. You may already be remembering to emanate gentleness from the centre of your body even. Nonetheless, the whole population of planet earth uses kidney-generated energy to motivate themselves. The mind says 'Come on!' or 'I had better set off now!' These thoughts race through the body and draw on the kidneys to stimulate a response. Kidney chi is not finite but neither can it be replenished. It is possible to go on using it, in the same way as it is possible to go on relying on our mental energy to organize ourselves and decide what is important and what is not. It is one dimensional, unhealthy and frenetic. Instead, you can bring grace and fluidity to your physical being in the world too. Allow the light of energy to impulse you, rather than ordering yourself about. The light informs your soul which elicits a response. This is delivered, or rather conveyed, via your lymphatic system. To support this process, try a bottle of Cleavers tincture, taken a few drops a day, and just feel your lymphatic system activate.

There are four stages to our evolvement. Initially, the victim stage where we think things are happening to us and we are in constant reaction. Then there is the manifestation stage where we realize that we can create anything and take responsibility for what is happening and go exploring a bigger, multi dimensional reality. Then there is the channel stage where we allow the bigger picture to speak through us, usually through our words, our music, our art and every other gift we are lucky enough to have a chance to cultivate. This is a great confidence-building stage as we realize that it is not us as individuals trying to think big, it is our ultimate potential and job to shine as much light on the world as possible. Then, finally, there is love. At this point, you have got your personality completely out of the way. You are expressing a synergy, a sympathetic resonance, by literally your presence. So, starting now, say no to drama and yes to love. Practice your words of affirmation, 'I will always be there for you!' Enjoy physical touch, great chemistry and lasting peace. Offer acts of service and pay attention to physical and emotional needs. Spend quality time and remember that any time spent in unity is quality time. Whatever we bring is a gift, be it an apparent good or bad, so remember you yourself are a gift too. Finding the depth of those acknowledgements in yourself ensures they will be reflected back in your life. Notice where you are in the four stages and move up a gear.

What is the extent of the positive change we can bring?
It will dawn on you fairly soon that we can change the whole entire world. Possibly, as well, we should be getting on with it as it might well be exactly why we are incarnated at this transitional moment in history. To this end, come up with a few initial meditations to spend a little time visualizing. For example, an image of there being food on everyone's table around the world; compassion and fairness in place of every instance of chaos and injustice. Healthy soil on every continent and clear water. Once you have uploaded these possibilities, send the vibrations down stream or out into an ocean. Any stretch of water is suitable.

Remain in, or get yourself into, if its unprecedented, a quiet receptive state and keep listening for whispers from the universe. There are sparks of inspiration, help and love everywhere. The more you hear them, the more you raise your frequency and enter the serenity of other dimensions. If that sounds a bit too ambient, I am really saying keep shifting your perspective until you see perfection. Stop filtering out the bigger picture and staying limited to an old dissatisfied viewpoint. I am not saying you were...but just in case you were.

Try and depersonalize your life mission. In a matter of decades at most, we will be gone and quickly forgotten. We are here to participate in a much bigger picture unfolding, called humanity. Visualize a humane world and a path of forgiveness through it ... and go for it. Do not get stuck in destructive ego limitations, thinking you need this or that before you move on. Have confidence that you do not need anything, you are everything already. As soon as you let it, your inner spirit will be guide enough. Spend your waking hours paying attention to the love and possibility that underlies every one of your life situations.

The End!

Acknowledgements

I would like to thank the people who have inspired me with their concepts and sometimes just their turn of phrase. In particular, the philosophers Peter Kingsley, Derek Walcott, Empedocles, Aristotle, George Bernard Shaw and William Desmond.

Thank you to those that have developed my compassion, Albert Einstein and the Saints, in particular Francis, Augustine and Germain. Nelson Mandela for his call to empowerment and Vimala Rogers for her means to respond to it. Also the musicians, Damien Dempsey, Lucinda Drayton, Ben Harper, JP Ryan, Stevie Nicks, Sandy Denny, Paolo Nutini and the mystic, Rumi.

I am grateful as well for the whole spectrum of films from the tragic Plague Dogs and Bleak Moments, to the grand scale of Star Wars and The Secret and deluded happily, in between, by many period dramas and the Bourne series.

Thank you to everyone who has illuminated my understanding of the energetic universe and facilitated my participation, in particular the work of bio-architect Michael Rice, Eric Dowsett, Barbara Hand Clow, Bruce Lipton, Dr. Emoto, Veronica, Margaret Denmead, Freya Lawton, Bart Heijting, Serge Benhayon and Lucy Pringle.

Made in the USA
Charleston, SC
13 August 2015